"This book will truly change your perception of God's ability to work the supernatural in you and through you! This timeless compilation of stories takes you on an amazing adventure of signs, wonders, and miracles communicated through many personal experiences. Not only has it compelled me to draw closer to God, but it has encouraged me to let God do the supernatural through me while relating to me on a very personal level!"

Pastor David Winston

"*From the Natural to the Supernatural* is a must-read, a true gem! It thrusts you on an adventure into the realm of the Supernatural like you have never experienced before. This book inspires you to close the door on the mundane Christian life and explode full force without seat belts into the supernatural realm of God's power, protection, and provision."

Love McPherson Gideon Group Chicago, IL

From the Natural *to the* Supernatural

True life stories...

Danielle DeMartino

Copyright © 2013. Danielle DeMartino

All rights reserved. No part of this book may be used or reproduced by any means, graphic, electronic, or mechanical, including photocopying, recording, taping or by any information storage retrieval system without the written permission of the publisher except in the case of brief quotations embodied in critical articles and reviews.

WestBow Press books may be ordered through booksellers or by contacting:

WestBow Press
A Division of Thomas Nelson
1663 Liberty Drive
Bloomington, IN 47403
www.westbowpress.com
1-(866) 928-1240

Because of the dynamic nature of the Internet, any web addresses or links contained in this book may have changed since publication and may no longer be valid. The views expressed in this work are solely those of the author and do not necessarily reflect the views of the publisher, and the publisher hereby disclaims any responsibility for them.

Any people depicted in stock imagery provided by Thinkstock are models, and such images are being used for illustrative purposes only.

Certain stock imagery © Thinkstock.

NKJV – New King James Version
Scripture taken from the New King James Version. Copyright 1979, 1980, 1982 by Thomas Nelson, inc. Used by permission. All rights reserved.

ISBN: 978-1-4497-1532-8 (sc)
ISBN: 978-1-4497-1533-5 (hc)
ISBN: 978-1-4497-1530-4 (e)

Library of Congress Control Number: 2011926430

Printed in the United States of America

WestBow Press rev. date: 1/24/2013

I want to dedicate this book to David and Niki for giving me the opportunity to write it. I am forever grateful. Also, I dedicate this book to my wonderful family for their encouragement and belief in me and the purpose to which I am called.

Contents

Introduction 1
An Encounter with Christ 5
Baby with Rare Blood Disease 13
Falling Through the Ice 19
My Friend's Final Days 23
The Lady in the Road 33
I Need a Sign 39
Gang Member Saved 45
Doug Go! 53
The Wrong Number or Not? 59
A Yorkie and a Herd of Cattle 63
On a Mission 67
The Girl in the Hotel 73
A Journey to Hell 81
Salvation Vacation 85
The Blind Man 95
An Hour to Live 101
Wife and Mother Diagnosed with Cancer 105
The Couple Who Wanted a Baby 113
The Road Trip 117
Spirits and Principalities 121
What Is a Demon? 125
Demons and Deafness 129
The Toddler That Drowned 133
Please Don't Let My Baby Die 137
In Conclusion 155

Introduction

Ephesians 3:20: Now to Him who is able to do exceedingly abundantly above all that we ask or think, according to the power that works in us.

The power of God was placed in us on the day we were saved. We have to put that supernatural power to work. In this verse we also see that it says, "to Him who is able to do exceedingly and abundantly above all that we ask or think." Not only will we get what we ask or think, but greatly, largely and breathtakingly above that. Praise God! We have an amazing "power source" within us called the Holy Spirit. When we allow the Holy Spirit to work through us, we have the supernatural power to overcome everything! The only thing the Holy Spirit needs is a natural, physical body to work through, and that is us. This is how important we are to the Kingdom of God!

1 John 3:8: For this purpose the Son of God was manifested, that He might destroy the works of the devil.

Jesus came as a man and worked with the power of God, through the Holy Spirit. When Jesus was crucified and died, He empowered us as believers to continue the work exceedingly and abundantly above all we could ask or think with a Helper called Holy Spirit.

> *John 14:16: And I will pray the Father, and He will give you another Helper, that He may abide with you forever.*

The Greek word used for "another" is *allos*. It means "another one exactly like me." "Helper" or "Comforter", *parakletos*, means, "One called alongside to help." He is in us working together with God in the person of the Holy Spirit.

It is not our physical appearance that makes us a powerful person. It doesn't make a difference if you are tall, have good stature, spend three thousand dollars on an Armani suit, or if you are wearing a Rolex watch and sporting snakeskin shoes. Neither God nor the devil is impressed with your physical attributes or your ability to sport expensive outfits. God and the Holy Spirit are looking for a dwelling place that they can operate and manifest their power through! So be encouraged to make your body a living sacrifice. God has given you His power!

> *1 John 4:4: He who is in you is greater than he who is in the world.*

We have the Greater One within us, greater than sickness, disease, death, demons, or poverty!

This book was written to encourage and exhort you to tap into that power. It is not you; it is God in you, working through you. You are the vessel, and He is the power source. We just need to get the revelation of that on the inside of us.

Start exercising your faith by believing, and you will find yourself able to tap into His power in every situation. We have an important purpose. God wants to use us to change this world.

> *Luke 10:19: Behold I give you the authority to trample on serpents and scorpions, and over all the power of the enemy.*

The Word says we have authority (dominion) over all the power of the enemy. The enemy has no power over us. We don't have to wait for Jesus to come floating down from heaven to give us the victory. We already gained the victory at the cross; we need to use our authority.

There is no reason Satan should have the ability to run over you, your family, your health, your finances, or your ministry. If he is running over you, it is because you have given him the ability to. Why do we allow a lower-ranking lieutenant to have authority over us? We need to train ourselves to believe beyond our natural ability and beyond our natural reasoning. We are spiritual supernaturally empowered beings first and foremost. We just live in a natural shell, but God needs our hearts, our hands, our feet, and our minds to do His Kingdom work here on earth. Power scares people, but if you're in fear, you're not in faith. Our prayer should be, "Plug me in, Lord, and use me to light up the world and do mighty works in Your name."

We are living in an era right now where God is stirring up the gifts inside each of us, but He requires faith and obedience from us. With that being said, the purpose of this book is to encourage, lift up, and equip believers to a level where we are supposed to be in our faith and gifts. These are true-life stories of natural persons performing supernatural things. I encourage anyone who reads this book to share it with others who may not be saved or who may need a healing or a miracle. Take a step of faith and be the vessel that God can use.

As this book takes you through a journey of true-life stories that are captivating and full of power, enjoy. Some of the names have been changed to protect the identity of others. The stories in this book are not necessarily in chronological order, but all are true and Scripture based.

I would like to thank my Heavenly Father for the supernatural power He has bestowed upon natural human beings called believers.

An Encounter with Christ

It was June 9, 1970, and I was sixteen years old. I had just come home from running away again. A few weeks earlier, my father had beaten my face until it was unrecognizable. When he was done doing me in, my blood was spattered all over the walls. Sobbing, I threw some of my clothes in a pillowcase, pitched it out my bedroom window, jumped out and ran. I was gone for well over a month.

When I arrived back home, my sister and I wanted to do something with our girlfriend Jenny. We piled into my sister's car and went to pick up Jenny to spend some girl time. We arrived at Jenny's home, where she ran up to the car and got in. I scooted over to the middle of the front seat, in between my sister Roseanne, who was driving, and Jenny on the passenger side. There were no seat belt laws back then, so the seat belts were usually buried in the crook of the seat and ignored.

We were driving along Montauk Highway, a single-lane highway in the town of Eastport, where I went for most of my high school years. We were gabbing away, the way teenage girls do, when suddenly Jenny screamed out, "A dog!" A dog ran out in front of the car, and we were going faster than we should have been. My sister's reaction was to quickly turn the steering wheel, and we slammed straight into a big oak tree. The sound of crushing metal and shattered glass resounded in my ears as we came to a halt. The front of the car was wrapped around the tree. Everything after that became vague.

I recall people yelling, "Get her out — the car is going to explode!" Someone opened the door and pulled me out. I was set down in someone's front yard. I went in and out of consciousness. I recall a crowd gathering and then I heard my mother's voice. She placed my head in her lap. She and my father made it there before the ambulance. They must have really booked, because the fire department was much closer than our home. I could hear my sister screaming in the background as they loaded Jenny and me onto backboards and lifted us up into the ambulance.

When I arrived at the hospital, my mom demanded a specialist. I don't remember much after that. Between the semi-consciousness and drugs, I was out of it. I was later informed I had received approximately 150 stitches in my face alone and suffered a traumatic brain injury. A chunk of flesh was gone from behind my right arm. Some of it could be stitched, but they had to fill the rest with gauze until the flesh grew in on its own.

Vaguely, I remember the corridor being jam-packed with my friends who had heard about the wreck. After I was sewn back together, I was wheeled out on the stretcher and everyone started to cheer. I hadn't realized the severity of my accident yet. It all seemed surreal.

I later found out that Jenny had some stitches on her chin where her teeth had gone through. My sister had only some bad bruising from the steering wheel. Thank God for that.

From the Natural to the Supernatural

I had gone through the windshield of the car, shattering the glass with my head and face.

As I was lying in the hospital bed, I could hear my mother outside the room asking questions about my condition. There was desperation in her voice. I heard them telling her that it was fifty/fifty, and they couldn't make any guarantees. We would just have to wait it out. My father came to my bedside and for the first time I ever remembered, he told me he loved me. I wanted to get up. I wanted to talk, but my body wouldn't move or listen to my commands. I wanted to tell my Mom, "I'm all right," but I couldn't speak. People were in and out of my room. Then it finally quieted down.

I began to feel like I was going into a deep sleep. All of a sudden, I could hear choirs of angels singing. I recognized these voices because as a little girl, after being terrorized with abuse, the angels' singing would come and comfort me.

I heard beautiful, melodic voices — no instruments. The singing was engulfing and brought comfort. *"How serene,"* I thought to myself. As I laid there in awe and peace at the same time, a wonderful light came into my room at the foot of my bed. In the next moment, I had lifted out of my body and was floating above it. I could see my shell lying in the bed. I heard the angels singing, saw the light and the body. As I looked down, I said to myself, "I must be dead. This is nice." It felt so peaceful. Then I thought, "What about my mom?" She would be so upset...but I liked where I was.

Suddenly, Jesus appeared out of the light that glowed in my room. "Jesus, it's You," I said. "Yes," He answered. As He looked at me, His eyes drew me into His love, like a magnet, unlike any love here on earth. It was safe, secure, unconditional, and all encompassing. He wore a white robe. It was illuminated, and within His robe there was glory, purity, and all that was holy.

> *Mark 9:2: Now after six days Jesus took Peter, James, and John, and led them up on a high mountain apart by themselves; and He was transfigured before them. V: 3: His clothes became shining, exceedingly white, like snow, such as no launderer on earth can whiten them.*

Then He spoke to me, "Your time has not yet come. Go and spread the word." Not one fiber of me wanted to stay in this natural world; I wanted to be with Him. This world dulled in His presence. "No!" I pleaded, "I want to go with You!" "You must go back and spread the word," He repeated. I floated and soaked in His presence for a while, and then my spirit was sucked back into my body. I wondered, "What is this 'word' I am supposed to spread?" Would it be one word like "love" or "peace" and something magical would happen to others when I said it? Would this word have mystical power? This started my quest.

Previous to this encounter, at the age of fourteen, I had been a self-proclaimed atheist and a vegetarian (which was very common for what we call the "hippie" era). Although I had been raised Catholic, I had no relationship with Jesus. Years of abuse by my dad made me hate God as a child. "God's punishing you," would be my father's words. "Great, I am being abused by my dad, and God is punishing me." I wondered what I had done as a timid, fearful child to deserve years of abuse, and why God always wanted to punish me as well. By the time I was ten, I would lay in my bed at night and say, "God, if You are really real, I hate You."

At fourteen, I decided there was no God and I was on a mission to spread my beliefs. I believed that we burst from an amoeba and over time morphed into human beings, but now, after the accident, I knew the truth. There was a God, He loved me, and I had a purpose. I just had to find it.

I rarely shared with others about my experience with Jesus. The few times I did, people thought perhaps I had lost my mind in the accident. I told my experience to my mom. She proceeded to tell me when people have accidents, they have bad dreams, "No, Mom, this wasn't a bad dream!" I declared. I told my closest friends. They just looked at me as if to say, "Girl, you have lost it!" To my surprise my sister Roseanne said, "I believe you." Yes! Those were the most comforting words she had ever said to me.

Within a year after the accident, I was up to my old ways, smoking pot and hanging with the wrong crowd. The devil was having a heyday as I turned to drugs and my drug family to soothe the pain of years of severe abuse.

Where are You, Jesus? Why is my life worsening? What have You to do with me? The questions always came up in my mind, but I was being pulled further down. The drugs were clouding my mind, allowing me to escape my past, but I never forgot about my time with Jesus.

> *Jeremiah 29:11-14 says, For I know the thoughts that I think toward you, says the Lord, thoughts of peace and not of evil, to give you a future and a hope. Then you will call upon Me and go and pray to Me, and I will listen to you. And you will seek Me and find Me, when you search for Me with all your heart. I will be found by you, says the Lord, and I will bring you back from your captivity.*

One day, Johnny, a friend of mine, said to me, "I have some really good pot. Let's smoke some and go to my sister Millie's house and make fun of her. She's a Christian." It sounded like a fun plan to me, so we set out on our journey, getting very high on the ride and shortly arriving at Millie's.

We got out of the car in this little middle class neighborhood. Giggling from our high, we proceeded to the front door. We knocked, Millie answered, and with a warm greeting, she invited us in. Johnny introduced me and her reaction was, "Danielle, it's so nice to meet you. I have heard so much about you. Would you like a cup of tea and some fresh baked cookies?" "That sounds great!" I replied, since the munchies had set in.

Millie made tea and served cookies and was loving and kind. She was so different from anyone I had ever met before. Her being was lit up with love. I did not want to make fun of her at all! I felt uncomfortable in my skin; conviction soaked my mind, body, and soul. What was this uncomfortable state I was in? Being high was no stranger to me. I just wanted to run and hide from the embarrassment as I sat at the table with this lady who was so full of love and light. No one made fun of Millie that day.

"Well, we have to get going," said Johnny. We got up, thanked Millie, and headed toward the door. I breathed a sigh of relief. Finally I can get away from the conviction that was overtaking me. I thought to myself, "I would like to come back and visit her again when I am not high." We said our goodbyes, and the door shut behind me. Then, all of a sudden, the door opened back up. It was Millie. "Danielle!" she shouted. I turned and said, "Yes?" "I have to obedient," Millie proclaimed, "God wants me to tell you something, and I must be obedient." I was stone cold stuck in my steps. "Oh no," I thought, "I am in trouble." She continued, "Jesus loves you and wants to take that marijuana away from you." "Oh… OK," I nervously replied. "Thank you." Johnny was giggling, but I felt so heavy with sin.

"Wow," I thought. That was the most embarrassing thing that I had ever experienced. How did she know I was high?" I felt like a child whose hand had got caught in the cookie jar. There was something very familiar about Millie. It was a glimpse of what I experienced when Jesus Himself stood before me. There was a light in her that drew me to her, and it was because she was a representative of Christ. I recognized Christ in Millie.

> *Matthew 5:16: Let your light so shine before men, that they may see your good works and glorify your Father in heaven.*

Those words from Millie would stay with me for the years that followed, as well as my encounter with Jesus Himself.

Baby with Rare Blood Disease

Six years later, after my encounter with Millie, I had been married and gave birth to a beautiful baby girl named Naydia. During a time when I was separated from her father, she had become terminally ill. She was diagnosed with a rare blood disease. The doctors had told me there were only seven cases known at that time, mostly in South America. They hadn't found a cure. I moved to Brooklyn, New York to be closer to a great blood specialist. Nay had spent many weeks at a time in the hospital. She was in an oxygen tent, holding onto life. She was a very good, quiet natured little girl, who was no doubt in the fight of her life. She barely ate. Much of her nourishment was through a feeding tube.

When she was born and handed to me, I felt like I had just received the best gift anyone could ever ask for, dream of, or imagine. Her hair was black and long at birth. Her eyelashes were thick, long, and lush. She was perfect. When I held her, I fell so in love and I thought to myself, "I am going to give her the life I never had." She was my constant and the tool used to change my life, and now…she was losing hers.

"She won't live to see the age of three," were the doctor's words that were coldly delivered to me. I was going to lose my baby. I stood there, frozen in time. "Why, God?" I asked. "Haven't I suffered enough? Now my baby is going to die?" The worse her condition got, the worse mine was as well. I had come off drugs when I got pregnant and committed to being the best mother in the world. Now the best thing that had ever happened to me was being taken away. Nay was fighting for her life and I was giving up on mine. I went to see the doctor for my nerves and anxiety. I was put on Valium. The Valium would numb the pain temporarily; however, I just wanted to die.

November 26, 1976, NayNay was almost two and a half years old. I had just picked her up from the hospital. When I got her, they had just taken blood work. I brought my beautiful little girl home to our new apartment on Avenue O in Brooklyn. I loved how she would lay her tiny little head on my shoulder and just rest. I could feel the love going back and forth through our bodies. I could stay there forever. She looked pale and exhausted. War was raging in her body fighting against itself to stay alive. I set her down on the couch and tried to make a little dinner. I peeked back at her a few minutes later, and I could see that familiar look. It was that look that said, "It's back to the hospital." "Not again! Please, God, not again," kept rolling through my mind. I looked over at the table, and on it sat a brand new prescription of Valium I had just filled. "I could bring NayNay back to the hospital and just take the whole prescription and end my life right now," I thought. "No, that would be so selfish of me to end my life before my little girl." I just started to cry out of control. Everything was out of control and my life was speedily in a downward spiral I wasn't scraping the bottom of the barrel — I was underneath it. How could I ever live without my baby?

As the tears soaked my shirt, I began to think back to the car accident and the hospital when the angels came singing. The light that came into my room, Jesus, and what he said to me. My thoughts raced to Millie, who six years previously told me Jesus loved me and wanted to take that marijuana away from me. "Maybe," I thought, "just maybe, Jesus would be willing to help me." In my darkest despair, right there, in the middle of my living room, on Avenue O in Brooklyn, New York, I dropped to my knees, and these were the words I spoke: "Jesus, I don't even know how to pray, but if You really love me, please don't let my baby die."

When I prayed that prayer something came over me from the top of my head and went down through my whole body. I felt washed clean from head to toe. It was a soaking. It was something I had never experienced before. I began to cry and purge all the years of pain, abuse, and torment. In exchange, I felt a peace that I could never explain with human words fill my soul. I knew God heard my prayer. My life was changed in an instant. No one knocked at my door with a pamphlet. No one brainwashed me with his or her words or belief system. No one recruited me into a religion. What I experienced was between Jesus and me! It was personal, and I was never going to be the same. I knew on the inside, my daughter was healed. We never went back to the hospital that night. My baby and I slept together, in my bed, all cuddled up. As I drifted off to sleep, I thought to myself, "I just want to feel this way when I awake."

The morning sun was peeking through my first floor apartment. The window had been supplied with bars in order to keep criminals out. As I blinked my eyes, there was my NayNay, right beside my pillow. She was patiently waiting for me to wake. She was sitting with her legs tucked up underneath her, which was the way she would always perch. "Hey, Baby," I said blinking away the stream of light. "Hot dog, Mommy," she said. "You want a hot dog?" I asked. She nodded, yes. I eagerly arose and fixed her a hot dog for breakfast. She ate the whole thing! When she was done, she looked at me and said, "Cheese." "Cheese it is," as I opened the fridge. She rarely asked for food, she was too weak to even chew at times. My baby girl got whatever she wanted that day. If she wanted steak and lobster, I would've done whatever I had to in order to fill her request. However a simple hot dog and a slice of cheese was her desire.

As I was getting her food, on the inside of me I felt wonderful. I felt cleansed, with the sense that I had a new lease on life. I looked out my barred windows. There was one tree on the corner and it looked so beautiful to me. I could hear all the birds chirping in Brooklyn. I picked up the phone and called my boss. I told him what happened. I asked if I could have the day off to be with my girl. He was happy for us and gave us his stamp of approval.

I dressed my girl up in a cute little dress. I put her in the stroller, and we took our first walk to the Avenue. I purchased her a stuffed Cookie Monster (which was Nay's favorite Sesame Street character). I found her a new pair of soft, Italian leather shoes that she was so excited about. For me I purchased a Bible to begin my new journey.

I no longer desired smoking, drugs, or the wrong kind of friends. Those desires were completely wiped away. My life was radically changed and NayNay's was too. Shortly after, I got a call from her doctor, and he said her blood work came back completely normal! "Would you like to come in and have me redo it?" He asked. I told him no, because I knew

Jesus healed her. "Praise the Lord!" he responded. "Praise the Lord," I said.

> *Isaiah 53:5: But He was wounded for our transgressions, He was bruised for our iniquities; the chastisement for our peace was upon Him, And by His stripes we are healed.*

NayNay never had another bad report with her blood work. Jesus healed her and made her whole! Both of our lives were changed forever.

This led to a life of supernatural divine appointments, which, only God could orchestrate.

Falling Through the Ice

After NayNay was healed and I got saved, the Lord reminded me of an encounter I had when I was young. This encounter made me realize His hand had always been on my life. I was just brainwashed to think God was out to get me, through my dad.

I was nine years old. It was a very cold, breezy day. The sun shined on this beautiful Long Island town in Center Moriches, New York. I had received a new pair of ice skates for Christmas. I was ready to put them to use. I had skated before in the beginner blades. The kind that had two sets of blades on each skate. They strapped on with a buckle around your shoe. These new skates were real "big kid" skates. I was ready to throw these babies on and go for a spin.

After much pleading, my siblings and I convinced our parents to take us to the lake to skate. When we arrived, my heart beat faster as I looked out at the children skating on the lake. They were spinning in circles and gliding backwards with ease. I couldn't wait to get out there and practice my new approaching skills. The Lake was large, we called it Moriches Lake, and rumor had it, that it was a bottomless lake. No one had ever been able to measure its depth. It was kind of a local mystery. Nevertheless, I couldn't wait to get my nine-year-old body on those pretty shiny silver blades and conquer my new adventure! I sat on the shore and laced my skates up nice and tight. I stood up and wobbled toward the icy shore. Carefully, I placed my first foot on the ice and then my second. Before I could even push off, I was wobbling back and forth. Flailing my arms and trying to balance my body to keep from falling, down I went. Repeating this process quite a few times, I began to look around and see if anyone was watching. With each painful fall came a new vigor to succeed. Finally, I was up and skating. My ankles felt like rubber. I spent most of the time bending them back and forth trying to center my blades.

I skated off to the middle of the lake, avoiding the small puddles that formed on the ice from the sunshine. I noticed some kids I recognized from my elementary school. I wanted so much to fit in, but I didn't have very much confidence. I was a bit inward and awkward around everyone for that matter. I was a quiet child, too scared to say anything in fear of a beating from my father. All I knew was to be quiet or be beat, and sometimes that didn't work either. Now I was about an hour and a half on my skates, getting better and more sure-footed. I glanced over at my sister and she was gliding along as well and interacting with the other kids. Roseanne was my polar opposite. I wished I were more like her when I was young. Dad beat her too, but not as often. I seemed to be his target victim in more cases than none. Roe was bolder and had a voice. As I was skating along, I heard a whistle. It was my father and he was whistling us in to let us know our time was up. All I could think was I had better get to shore as soon as possible. If I didn't, I knew what my destiny would be. In my fury to get from point A to point B, I decided to skate through one of those watery patches. I was right in the middle of the lake at this point.

As I started my journey through the puddle, something unfathomable to my nine-year-old mind happened. I was wearing a ski jacket, sweater, skates, and all the gear when I disappeared through the ice, right in the center of the bottomless lake. The weight of my clothing and skates were bringing me down. I was frantically fighting under the icy water to get to the top but couldn't. In my terror, I began to swallow water. I was fighting and raging to save myself. Eventually, I became weakened and my energy gave out. I could feel my body become loose. As I began to drown, I could see beautiful colors. My life was flashing before my eyes and I could hear my mother's voice. She was crying.

Was this it? Is this how I was meant to go? So young? I began to pale more and give up the fight. Then all of a sudden a saw a huge arm came down. It was swishing around the water as though it was searching for me. Swish, swish. I was watching it, as I drifted downward.

All of a sudden this massive hand grabbed my hair at the top of my head. It began to pull me toward the surface. The hand brought me up until I could begin to see the light of day through the water. Next thing I knew, I was up out of the hole. He placed me on my side on the ice. Motionless, I laid there too weak to move. I watched this tall elderly man turn and walk away. I gazed at my hero as he just faded away and then vanished. I coughed up water and my body shivered as I lay. Within moments, my mother and father were by my side. The ambulance arrived and a fire truck was on the scene. They loaded me onto a stretcher and began to cut my clothes off. "No!" I screamed, "Don't cut my clothes off!" I began to cry out of embarrassment and shock. I had water in my lungs. They watched me for possible pneumonia to set in, but it didn't. All I could think about was the fading image of my hero.

No one saw the man I described. I am convinced he was my protective angel that God used to save me that day. My father began to tell people it was he who saved me so he could get attention. He knew well it was not he. I didn't correct him, being afraid of his wrath, but I knew it was my angel.

> *Psalm 91:11, 12: For He shall give His angels charge over you… In their hands they shall bear you up.*

As God's children, we are assigned bodyguards, sometimes one, and sometimes many. Whatever the situation is that we are in, God sends as many as we need. God wasn't done with me at nine years old. Even if the devil tried to finish me off, God's protection was over me. Think of how many times you had a brush with death or danger and somehow, supernaturally, you survived it. That is God and His angels fulfilling their assignment. God definitely does not put evil upon us, but He delivers us from it. He uses it to let us know we have a purpose to fulfill. These experiences are also called testimonies that we are to share with others to build their faith in God.

> *Revelations 12:11: And they overcame him by the blood of the Lamb and by the word of their testimony.*

There is power in your testimony. Don't hide your light under a bushel.

My Friend's Final Days

Joyce and I met years ago, in the late 1970s, through her son, who was a friend of mine. We became very close very fast. Sometimes there are those relationships where you just click and there is an instant bond. That is how it was with Joyce and me. She owned a chain of women's clothing stores with very nice upscale fashions. I had done modeling in my past, and I became a model for her fashion shows. At the time, I had two small children, and Joyce was very fond of them. They were fond of her as well. She was like a sister to me. Her smile would light up a room. She wasn't feeling well and was having some symptoms that were causing concern. She was later diagnosed with lung cancer. Joyce was a fighter, and she fought harder than anyone I had ever known. It was one of the hardest things I had ever experienced. Watching my beautiful, classy friend lose her appetite, lose weight, and lose her hair. It was heartbreaking. She kept on running the business. Joyce would pop on a turban style hat and go at it. She was also an avid golfer. If Joyce wasn't at the clothing store or at home, she was at the golf course.

As time passed, she became weaker and weaker. Soon she was on complete bed rest while undergoing aggressive chemo treatments, which left her nauseous and completely exhausted. It was hard to watch her go from this vibrant beautiful woman to a frail, shriveled little lady. This horrible rapidly growing disease was ravishing my friend, a woman who at one time had so much class and beauty.

I was saved about three years before I met Joyce. I was always looking for the perfect moment to tell her about Jesus, but we were always interrupted…isn't that just like the devil. I knew her salvation was vital and there wasn't much time. Typically, witnessing wasn't a problem for me, but every time I would start to witness, the enemy would come in and cause a distraction. I was filled with a sense of urgency regarding the importance of her salvation.

I spent hours every day with Joyce at her home. Sometimes the girls and I would spend the night at her house because she was left alone a lot. The highlight of her day was when my girls would go to her bedroom to visit. They would jump in the bed with her and snuggle. Joyce would smile from ear to ear. The girls would chat with her and listen to her stories. Then they would all fall asleep and take a nap together. One day my girls caught flu, and Joyce was not supposed to be around anyone sick in her frail condition. I put my girls in the car and we headed home. That flu was an attack from the devil. We dealt with fever, sick stomach, sore throat, and congestion. In the meantime, we couldn't be with Joyce for days. Well, she took a turn for the worst and was rapidly going downhill. I called my friend Luddy from church and told her of Joyce's condition. There wasn't much time and something had to be done now! Luddy, being the faithful Baptist lady she was, said, "Well, let's go right now then." I picked Luddy up and we were on our way to Joyce's house. She had no problem with being in bed around me, but she never met

Luddy. She was too much of a lady to have a stranger meet her for the first time in a bedroom She managed to muster up the energy to put on her turban and a robe and sit in the living room with us.

At first the conversation was a little strained. Luddy and I had an agenda for sure and Joyce had no idea what it was. We were chatting, and knowing Luddy, she was looking for that perfect place in our conversation to bring up Jesus. I was filled with anticipation and was praying internally that Joyce would accept Jesus. Then Luddy, the feisty elderly lady that she was, took things into her own hands and blurted out, "So how long have you had cancer?" Joyce being as gracious as she was replied, "For about a year now." "Well, you need Jesus then, don't you?" Luddy continued. I was at the edge of my seat, my heart was racing, and my mind was going at a thousand miles a minute. I wondered what might be going through Joyce's mind at this point. She just smiled at Luddy. "Let me tell you about Jesus," Luddy continued. "OK", replied Joyce.

Luddy was from the south with a strong southern accent. She was always bold and to the point. I met Luddy one day shortly after I was divorced from my children's father. I was living in the middle of Heath, Kentucky, at the time. I was alone to raise two little girls by myself. I was saved, but at the time, I was backsliding. I had gone through a divorce and walked off of God's path. Because of my weak faith, I gave the enemy the opportunity to have power over me. I knew Jesus was my Lord, but my lack of faith made me vulnerable. I was in a battle to survive, provide for my children, and be a single mom in the middle of nowhere. I felt very alone. I prayed to God for help and strength to care for my children. I was dealing with an issue in my body as well.

A knock came on my door. "Who could that be?" I wondered. I had just moved in the middle of the country, and I knew no one here. I answered the door, and there stood before me this cute little elderly lady and a teenage boy. "Hello, I'm Luddy and this is Sam. We were just coming through the neighborhood and wanted to welcome you," she said. "Neighborhood? What Neighborhood?" I thought to myself. I hadn't seen another house for a half a mile around here. "May we come in?" she asked. I was not in the mood for company. I had been in tears just minutes before she arrived and it was quite evident. Luddy stood there with this adorable, expectant look on her face and I couldn't refuse. "Oh sure, come on in." I replied. "Sure is a beautiful day out today. Have you seen this weather?" she boasted. "Weather, who cares about the weather," I thought. I was in a muck, and on top of it I had just received a bad report from my doctor. I had an issue in my body, and it required surgery that would keep me in the hospital for a week. I didn't know anyone who could keep my children, and the doctor wanted to get me in surgery as quickly as possible. I was very particular about who my children stayed with. As a young girl, I had encountered some pretty sick human beings, one of them being my own father. I had become very protective over my children. I knew well that all it takes is one sick offense against a child, and it could rob them of their whole childhood, affecting them throughout their adult life.

Luddy and Sam were now sitting at my kitchen table. I asked them if they would like a drink. Water was their only request. I took a seat at the table. Luddy said, "We just like to stop by and welcome people into the neighborhood to see if you have any needs we can help you with." I was hesitant, but I decided to be honest. "I could use some prayer actually.

I am scheduled for surgery in three days, and I don't have anyone I trust to care for my girls," I blabbed out. Then I began to cry…hard! I am now crying out of control and at the same time thinking, "Pull it together, Danielle. You are bawling in front of strangers you met three minutes ago." This was very out of character for me. Luddy got up from her seat, walked over to me, and grabbed my hands, pulling me up to a standing position. She put her arms around me and held me in a bear hug. "There, there now, don't you worry about a thing. We are going to pray and believe God that His hand is on this situation." I was now in a full-blown purging cry, soaking Luddy's shirt. Sam tried to comfort me as well by patting me on my back. Luddy just continued to hold me until I calmed down. We broke our hold, and Luddy stepped back and said, "Look at me." I stepped back and looked back at her in my pitiful state. "Everything is going to be all right. Do you understand?" she said with confidence. I nodded yes. I was unable to speak, and if I did, I would just break down every time I tried. Luddy took my hands and she, Sam, and I prayed for God to work out every detail. We gave it over to God; now it was off of me, and unto Him. They waited until they thought they were done. Luddy took my phone number so she could check up on me. When I closed the door behind them, although feeling a bit foolish, I knew God sent them. They were members of a local Baptist church, and they invited me to visit. It would have to be after the surgery, but I accepted the invite.

After my visit with Luddy and Sam, I was in the living room having a tea party with my daughters. They had a mini tea set I had bought them. They just thought it was the greatest thing to serve tea and cookies. It made them feel like grownups. I must admit, I enjoyed them being so adorable.

It took my mind off of the things that had laid heavy on my heart. I felt a sense of peace after praying with Luddy and Sam. I can't even imagine what this teenage boy must have been thinking when I broke down and babbled like a baby. He had so much compassion. You know, sometimes as Christians we go through valleys. Sometimes God uses other believers to come along to lift up and encourage us. I was always the strong one, the person others looked up to. It was hard for me to let down my guard and open up with someone. We can be dodging bullets in the natural, and sometimes we need to recruit other soldiers to join us and help fight the battle using the Word of God and prayer.

The phone rang about an hour and a half after they left, and it was Luddy. "Hey, good news," she boasted. "Oh yeah? What's the good news?" I asked. "Well, our pastor and his wife have five kids and an English Sheepdog. They are going to take your youngest daughter when you go to the hospital. The Deacon and his wife, have two teenager daughters, are going to take your oldest daughter!" She exclaimed. "What? Are you kidding me?" I said in amazement. "No, I am not kidding. They are great folks, and your girls will be safe and well taken care of!" she said excitedly. "Wow! Luddy, seriously, you are a godsend." The next day Luddy picked me up and took me to the pastor's house to meet him and his family. They were lovely, God-fearing people. Then we were off to Deacon Benny's home, and I loved them as well. I had a peace that it was all a part of God's plan. My girls would be safe; I knew it by the witness of the Holy Spirit on the inside.

I had the surgery, and when I woke from anesthesia, sitting by my side was Joyce. "Hey, Joyce, what are you doing here? You should be resting," I said. "I wasn't going to let you go through this and not be here for you," she replied. "Aww…

thank you," I mumbled and drifted off. When I completely gained my senses, Joyce was gone. I noticed flowers from the church, and Luddy and Sam came to visit.

When I returned home, the church had made a schedule of homemade meals. They were delivered to my house until I was up and around. I started attending the church when I was able to get out and about. I was blessed to have this wonderful family in Christ. The love that dwelled there and the heart of the evangelist that was upon that congregation was wonderful. My faith was restored, and I was back on track with God. Luddy and I became close and would enjoy tea, lunch, and running errands together over the months. Now we were together on a mission to get my friend who had been stricken with cancer saved.

Luddy went on to tell Joyce about Jesus and why He came to earth of His own free will. She explained to her that He came to be the ultimate sacrifice for our sins. Luddy continued to witness telling about the crucifixion and the blood Jesus that was shed so that we could be forgiven.

> *Romans 5:8: But God demonstrates His own love toward us, in that while we were still sinners, Christ died for us.*

She explained that it was His desire to be in relationship with us and when we ask Him into our heart, He becomes our Lord and Savior. Joyce listened intently. "When you belong to Him, you are guaranteed eternal life with Him in heaven." Then Luddy said, "Would you like to ask Jesus into your heart, Joyce?" "Yes, I would very much like to do that," she responded.

> *John 1:12: But as many as received Him, to them He gave the right to become children of God, to those who believe in His name.*

Luddy led her in the prayer of salvation.

> *Romans 10:9:...if you confess with your mouth the Lord Jesus and believe in your heart that God has raised Him from the dead, you will be saved. For with the heart one believes unto righteousness, and with the mouth confession is made unto salvation.*

Tears streamed down her face as she repeated the prayer of salvation. When we finished praying, Joyce said, "This is the best I have ever felt." God touched her that day and changed her destiny. She was glowing as the Spirit of the Lord rested upon her.

> *Romans 10:13: For "whoever calls on the name of the Lord, shall be saved."*

We then prayed for her healing. We all hugged, and Joyce went back to bed to rest.

Luddy and I were in the car driving home, thrilled about what God had just done. My heart was filled with joy. Now I knew my dear friend was saved.

A few days later, I found out Joyce was flying to Texas for a new more aggressive treatment. She had left a message on my answering machine that went like this, "Hey, where are you? I am headed out to Texas in the morning. I need to talk to you." I dialed her back; she told me she had so much peace in her heart since she asked Jesus to be her Lord and Savior. She wanted to know if I could come by. She said she had something to share, something between her and me and a third person. I couldn't come by that night. I didn't have a sitter and my car was in for repairs. I prayed for her, and we said goodbye.

She left for Texas in the morning. That would be the last time I would talk to her. Joyce went home to be with Jesus while in Texas. I have always wondered what it was that she wanted to tell me before she passed, who the third person was that she spoke of. On the inside, I think she knew she was going home and that third person was the Lord. I missed her so much after she passed, but she is in my future. I cannot wait until we talk again. God is good, and His mercy endures forever. My friend is in Heaven in a glorified body, no more suffering.

The Lady in the Road

It was a typical day at home with my two girls. NayNay was seven years old at the time, and Niki was three. The phone rang, and it was my sister Laureen. She asked if I wanted to go to the mall shopping. It sounded like a great idea and nice way to spend time with my sister. "I will meet you at the library at 10 AM. Don't be late. If you are, I am going without you," she chuckled, but she meant it at the same time.

I was trying so hard to get the girls and me ready but was distracted by what took place the night before. I had just drifted off to sleep when I was awakened by an audible voice that said, "Be obedient and listen to my voice!" My eyes popped open, and I looked around to see if someone was in my bedroom. No one except my husband was there, and he was fast asleep next to me. I closed my eyes again and began to drift off to sleep. Again the voice came, repeating itself, "Be obedient and listen to my voice!" I sat up immediately, looked around, and then bent over to take a closer look at my husband's face. He was definitely sleeping. "What the heck was this voice?" I wondered. Finding it hard to fall back to sleep, I finally began to doze off. Once again the voice spoke even louder and bolder, "Be obedient and listen to my voice!"

Eyes wide open and looking toward Heaven, I said, "OK, Lord, I will do whatever You tell me to do! I promise!" After that, I waited for more instruction, but nothing came. It was a good hour before I could drift off to sleep again.

It seemed no matter how hard I tried to get the girls and me ready, I just wasn't able to move fast enough. The library was only blocks away. My sister's words were ringing in my head. "If you're late, I am leaving without you!" Finally, I got everyone loaded in the car ten minutes late. I was anxious to get there as soon as I could. I turned to the right, out of my driveway and onto the bypass to take the short cut. The bypass did not have a lot of traffic, except during rush hour.

I was approaching the first intersection when, from a distance, I could see something large lying in the right lane. I thought this large object was trash that fell from someone's truck or a heaping piece of furniture. As I approached and got a clearer look, I could see that it was a body! Then the voice came back, "Pull over!" But Lord, what am I supposed to do?" "Pull over!" I heard again. It was brought to my remembrance the night before when He commanded me to be obedient and listen to His voice. I pulled over, and now my three-year-old daughter, Niki, was screaming with fear at the sight of the lifeless woman on the road. She had never seen anything such as this. NayNay just stared out the window at this woman heaped in a pile. "Get out of the car!" the Lord said.

I opened my door and began to approach the body. I knelt on the pavement next to her. She was a large elderly woman, and I heard her gurgling. Having gone to nursing school, I knew how to check for vitals, so I did. No heartbeat. No breathing. I looked around and noticed that her shoes had been thrown off her feet. Her watch and necklace were scattered in the street. Her body was not in a natural position.

A pool of blood from her head flowed across the road and formed a little puddle where the street sloped down. The woman's clavicle bone was broken and rose out of her back, like a small mountain. This lady was dead, but what had happened? Looking around, I didn't see a car or anything that could indicate how this accident could have occurred.

Kneeling there, I wasn't sure what I was supposed to do, then the voice came again, "Tell her to live and not die." Now I had read in the Bible where Jesus had raised people from the dead. I never had, nor had I known a person who had at this point in time. Again, thinking of those words He spoke to me the night before, I laid my hand on her back and commanded, "Live and not die, in Jesus name!" As soon as I spoke those words, her clavicle bone went back into its natural position. A deep breath came into her lungs, and she began breathing. It startled me so much that I just put both of my hands on her and began to pray in the Spirit. I had just received the baptism of the Holy Spirit two months before.

Matthew 10:27: "Whatever I tell you in the dark, speak in the light; and what you hear in the ear, preach on the housetops."

As I prayed, I felt as though I had entered another dimension. I was unaware that the ambulance and a fire truck had arrived. The next thing I remembered was someone kneeling next to me. He was a medic. He said, "What are you doing?" "Praying," I answered. He began to pray with me. I glanced over and noticed it was a gentleman I had attended high school with. He was a believer as well.

I arose to let the EMTs do their work. Looking around I noticed her car on the far left side of the bypass. It had crashed into trees, and the back window was out. Somehow, she ejected through the back window. The trees hid her car; you could barely see it in the thicket. I walked over to the firemen who were on the scene and pointed out the car. They thanked me. I walked toward my car. It was parked near an embankment that rose up to a high hill. I could see and hear my daughter Niki still screaming.

I looked up and on top the hill there was a house on the corner of the intersection. Behind the house was a barn and sticking out of the barn was a city bus. The barn lay in pieces where the bus had entered and crashed. Then I figured it out: the woman and the bus hit each other and ricocheted in opposite directions. I began to walk up the hill and felt a supernatural strength come over me. Just like Wonder Woman, I threw the boards and planks of the broken barn out of my way to get to the bus. When I was inside the barn, I noticed the bus door was open. I stepped in, and behind the wheel sat the driver. He was motionless, staring forward, his ear sliced and hanging, his face badly bruised. He was in shock.

I took a quick walk through the bus to see if there were any passengers, and there were none. I returned to the driver. "Sir? Can you hear me?" he nodded. "Do you know you were in an accident?" He nodded again. "I am going to go get you some help. You are going to be fine, but I have a question. If you were to have died today, do you know if you would have spent eternity with God in Heaven?" He turned and looked at me and said, "No I don't." "Would you like to have that assurance?" I asked. "Yes," he replied. "Do you believe that Jesus Christ is the Son of God, shed His blood, and died for your sin?" "Yes," he answered. "Do you believe He rose again and sits at the right hand of the Father in Heaven?" Another yes. "Then repeat after me: Jesus, I believe You died on the cross for me. Forgive me of my sins. Come into my heart and be my Lord and Savior. I dedicate my life to You now. Heal me, in Jesus' precious name I pray, Amen."

Matthew 10:32: "Therefore whoever confesses Me before men, him I will also confess before My Father who is in heaven."

We prayed together as tears flowed down his cheek. I explained to him that the angels in Heaven were rejoicing. His name was being written in the Lamb's book of life and he would spend eternity in Heaven. He felt comforted and peaceful. I then explained I was going for help. He thanked me. His life was changed forever.

I ran back down the hill. They were now loading the woman into the ambulance. I pointed out the bus and told them about the bus driver. They turned to look at the situation. They called for another ambulance. The EMTs ran to his aid.

I headed to my car. I calmed my little girl down, telling her that God sent us there to help. Niki was good with that explanation, and we headed to the library. In my mind was an internal conversation with God. "What was all that about?" I asked. "Being obedient and listening to My voice," said the Lord. If I hadn't been obedient, the woman would be dead and the bus driver would not be saved. Glory to God! He used a common little housewife and mother such as myself to perform two miracles in less than a half an hour. Isn't that just like God? I learned a valuable lesson about obedience that day.

I finally made it to the library, and my sister was frustrated. "I told you to be on time. I was just getting ready to leave without you," she rattled out. "Laureen, you will not believe what God just did!" I exclaimed. I told her the story, and all she could say was, "Praise God." That day I was impacted with the realization that we were created to do great things for God, the same things Jesus did. We are supernaturally empowered to do, through the Holy Spirit who dwells in us.

The woman lived. The bus driver survived his injuries, and God had my obedience.

> *Matthew 10:1, 7, 8: And when He had called His twelve disciples to Him, He gave them power over unclean spirits, to cast them out, and to heal all kinds of sickness and all kinds of disease. And as you go, preach, saying, "The kingdom of heaven is at hand." Heal the sick, cleanse the lepers, raise the dead, cast out demons. Freely you have received, freely give.*

I Need a Sign

The Lord spoke to me in 1981 and told me I was to go to Bible school. I told Him I would be obedient. Being the mom of two young daughters, I asked the Lord if I could wait until my girls were out of high school before I applied to a Bible school. It was 1993 when the Lord started preparing me. I had been involved with youth ministry, Woman's Aglow, and the Christian school for many years. I considered every day of my life a ministry, always "keeping my spiritual antennas up."

I owned a decorating/wallpapering company. It had taken years to build that very successful business. I knew if I were to start up a new company in a new town, I would hardly have time to work it and be a good student. I needed something that I could do part time and make a good amount of money as well.

In 1977 I attended cosmetology school in Kentucky. I inquired about my hours and renewing my license so I could get reciprocity in New York State. I had waited so many years that they weren't transferable; they couldn't even be found because of the time lapse. I would have to start all over again. Now I am praying, "Lord, what do I do? How will I support myself?" I had the idea of going back to cosmetology school in New York, getting my license, and applying for reciprocity in Oklahoma, where I would attend Rhema Bible Training Center. I had to know it was God! I weighed my options, prayed, and went through other possibilities. I kept coming back to cosmetology.

I was very concerned and wanted to be led on what to do. This was a big commitment, and although there was a grant involved, I still would have out of pocket expenses. I wanted to go full time but had to make sure I had enough to pay the bills. "God will provide," I reminded myself.

I had communicated with the office administrator of the Hairstyling Institute several times, Mr. Will, who was short and frank with me on the phone. He told me my options. When I had another question come up, I was hesitant to call. I felt like a bother to Mr. Will; he was so brief and stern in our communication. However, I needed some answers, and I had to pray this out.

Finally I decided: I would go and talk with the office about their program. Maybe then I would know something on the inside of me. I had to know this was God's plan. I had made enough plans of my own in my life that had always ended up with stress, anxiety, and sometimes failure, but I learned to live in God's grace. Now, I had become a mature Christian woman. I knew better than to make a decision without the Father's approval.

> *Proverbs 3:5, 6: Trust in the Lord with all your heart, And lean not on your own understanding; In all your ways acknowledge Him, and He shall direct your paths.*

I opened the door to my car that day to go to the school. Sitting behind the wheel I said to the Lord, "I have been praying about this for weeks and nothing. I need to know something!" I pleaded. I began my journey to the school a little apprehensively with, "Oh, Lord, I don't want to make a mistake," as I let out a sigh. I pulled into the parking lot of my destination and sat frozen in my car. One last prayer, "Lord, I don't mean to fleece You, but I need a sign that I am doing the right thing. Please, just give me a sign." I opened the door and stepped out of my car.

As I entered the school, an array of things were going on. Students were working on clients, some on mannequins, some on nails and answering phones. I thought to myself, "I have to do this all over again." An instructor approached me. "Can I help you?" she asked. "Yes, I am here to see about possibly becoming a student," I replied. She directed me to the back of the room, last door on the left.

I gently knocked on the door and peeked inside. There sat Mr. Will. "Hi, I am Danielle DeMartino. I have called and inquired about the school." "Yes, I remember you. You will be talking with Miss B.," he said coldly. I looked over in the direction he pointed to; a glass wall separated the two of them. Mr. Will's desk faced forward and her desk faced Mr. Will's.

I breathed a sigh of relief when I found out it was Miss B. I would be chatting with, and not Mr. Will. I didn't take it personally. It was just his disposition. Still the same, I was glad it was she I had to communicate with.

Miss B. was kind and had me sit down so I was facing her. Now Mr. Will was behind my back, but he was in Miss B.'s eyeshot. We began to talk about the school and its program, the hours and grants. As we spoke, I heard a thud! Miss B. got this horrified look on her face; she stood up and screamed out, "Mr. Will!" I turned around, and Mr. Will was out cold on the concrete floor by the copy machine.

Now Miss B. was screaming, "Get Mr. Richards! Get Mr. Richards!" as she ran out of the room. I walked over to Mr. Will's body; he was lying on his back. I had heard his head hit the floor, like a bat hitting a ball. His face and lips were blue, and he began to get a death gurgle. Miss B., Mr. Richards and others were now in the room "Call 911!" they shouted. "Call 911!" "He's dying!" screamed Miss B. Mr. Will looked very bad, definitely dying. With all the commotion around me, I felt incredibly calm and a peace came over me. I checked for a pulse and breath. There was nothing. At this point his lips were a purplish black. I knelt by Mr. Will's head and commanded, "You shall live and not die, in Jesus' name!" I tucked my hand behind his neck to clear his airways, and suddenly, he took a deep breath. Then came another breath and another.

> *Matthew 11:5, 6: "The blind see and the lame walk; the lepers are cleansed and the deaf hear; the dead are raised up and the poor have the gospel preached to them. And blessed is he who is not offended because of Me."*

"The ambulance is on its way!" they shouted. Miss B. and Mr. Richards stood in amazement as Mr. Will went from the color of death back to the color of life. His eyes finally opened, and he asked, "What happened?"

"What happened! You died is what happened!" shouted Miss B.

In the midst of all these unbelievers, God just performed a miracle!

We helped Mr. Will stand to his feet. He was a little woozy and he had a big knot on the back of his head where he hit the floor. Although he resisted, they took him to the hospital. I looked over at Miss B., who looked more shaken than Mr. Will. I caught her eye and said, "I will call you tomorrow, and we can continue then." She agreed. As I walked through the school, there was a look of shock on all the students' and instructors' faces.

I reached the back door, walked to my car, and climbed in. As I sat there for a moment, I thought to myself, "What in the world was that all about?" astonished at the death and life experience. Dazed, I slipped the key in the ignition, turned my car on, and then it hit me! There was my sign! I was needed there. Not just to go to school, but for others. Thank You Lord! I had hoped no one told Mr. Will his toupee fell off when he went down. I chuckled as peace filled my soul and I started my journey home.

I received my grant and started cosmetology school a few weeks later. My first day in the classroom, Mr. Will came in to give some paperwork to my instructor. Before he left, he turned, looked at me, and said, "I'm still alive!" "Yes, you are," I confirmed. The whole school knew the story, which led the students to ask me about my faith, and I was able to bring students to Christ through that experience.

> *Matthew 5:16: Let your light so shine before men, that they may see your good works and glorify your Father in heaven.*

I was thankful to God for my sign and for raising Mr. Will from the dead

Gang Member Saved

There was an opportunity in 1999 to go on a mission trip to Honduras with a missionary from Tulsa, Oklahoma. Several well-known ministers were joining him and a team of missionaries. We were to take a learjet from Tulsa airport. I have always had a heart for mission work, even before I got saved, so I tried to take every God-led opportunity I could.

It was communicated to us that we would be assigned to a church to preach while we were there. In my mind, I was imagining all the souls that would be won in Honduras. The anticipation of healings and miracles that would take place and all the churches that would be encouraged was creating such an excitement within my spirit. Little did I know that God was going to perform a miracle on the flight, in the learjet.

We all met at the airport in Tulsa that morning. There were familiar and unfamiliar faces. The faith level was high. There was a sense that we were all ready and prayed up. We were excited to experience what God was going to perform in Honduras.

It was time to board. After walking up the steps to our jet, I headed down the aisle of the plane. I searched for a seat.

A young man was sitting by himself. He was quite young, a teenager at most. He was wearing jeans and a tee shirt that had the arms cut off.

Not your typical looking missionary. Looking over at him I asked, "Do you mind if I sit here?" "No, not at all," he replied. I put my stuff under the seat and settled in. I clipped in my seat belt then turned to introduce myself. "Hi, I am Danielle," I said, reaching out my hand to welcome a handshake. He put out his hand to welcome mine and said, "I'm Herbie." "Nice to meet you," we said simultaneously.

I must admit, I was curious about Herbie. I admired the fact that he was so young and knew he wanted to do missions. I had wished that I had that kind of direction at his tender age. I noticed a scar on his arm that appeared to have been burned into his flesh. It looked like a brand you would burn into a horse or cattle signifying that they were one's property. My curiosity overcame me; I pointed to his scar and asked him what it signified. Herbie went on to tell me he was in a gang and he was sixteen years old. Herbie's mother and father were Christians, but Herbie went down the wrong path. He chuckled and continued to tell me how his mother put him on this mission trip in hopes that he would turn his life around. He said he looked at the trip as a free vacation on a learjet. Herbie shook his head like his mom's plan would not work.

As I sat there taking all of this in, I thought, "Ah…now I know why I was seated next to this young man…a praying momma got me here." I just love praying mommas and the heart they have toward their children. Mothers are self-sacrificing, putting their children before the Lord in prayer, believing for an intervention. Moms hit their knees before God to save their sons and daughters. They wake in the night when their children aren't in their beds sleeping. When they are out with their cohorts, looking for trouble, Momma prays. I spent many hours on my knees for my daughters, and God answered my prayers.

Herbie's Mom had to come up with the money for this trip. Her only prayer and agenda was for her son to get saved and turn his heart to Christ. Herbie chuckled again. "I mean, I love my mother, but this is just a glorified vacation," he boasted. "Well, he doesn't know whom he is sitting next to," were my only thoughts. He was sitting next to a praying Momma who is an evangelist and has a heart for youth. What a perfect scenario for God to move. My internal conversation with the Lord began, "Father open the door and give me the words you want me to speak only, that this boy would come to know You as his Lord and Savior."

Herbie and I hit it off! We were gabbing away. What I was doing was laying my foundation for trust from him toward me. Finally the release: I felt led to share with Herbie my testimony. I told him how I had a life filled with every kind of abuse from my father and how I turned to the wrong crowd for friends. I told him of the many drugs that I had taken. He shared with me his experiences as well. We found common ground: drug use, running, escaping, self-soothing with the wrong elements and the wrong friends. I shared with him how I had been an atheist at sixteen, same age as he. I now had Herbie's full frontal attention as we talked and shared. I told him of how I finally hit rock bottom, hopeless and suicidal after my daughter was diagnosed with a rare blood disease. He was captivated. "Herbie, I dropped to my knees and said a simple prayer that went like this: Jesus, if You love me, please don't let my baby die. In an instant, my whole life changed. I had been washed clean, my sin fell off of me, my spirit renewed, and my daughter was healed by a miracle," I testified.

"Really?" Herbie's eyes were wide open, in awe of the testimony of what God had done. "Yup!" I said. I opened up my Bible and began to read

> *John 3:16: For God so loved the world that He gave His only begotten Son, that whoever believe in Him should not perish but have everlasting life.*

I explained to him that Jesus took our sins on the cross that day so we could be forgiven, Herbie's jaw dropped, he was smiling with his perfect white teeth, his smile was one that would light up a room when he entered. Then I read from Romans.

> *Romans 10:9, 10: that if you confess with your mouth the Lord Jesus and believe in your heart that God has raised Him from the dead, you will be saved. For with the heart one believes unto righteousness, and with the mouth confession is made unto salvation.*

"So you see, Herbie, if you believe in your heart and confess with your mouth, you will be saved." Now Herbie's eyes were as big as potholes. "Do you want to know Jesus?" I asked. "Yes, I do," he answered, "Well, I am going to lead you in prayer right here, right now and you just repeat after me." OK, he nodded. "Dear Heavenly Father, I thank You for Your son Jesus. Jesus, I believe You shed Your blood for me. Forgive me of my sins, come into my heart now, and be my Lord and Savior." We ushered Herbie into the Kingdom of God right there in the air, on a learjet headed to Honduras. Herbie got radically saved and kept repeating, "I feel great! This is great! I have chills!" "That's the Holy Spirit," I explained. "He now lives on the inside of you and will never leave you."

All of a sudden, he stopped in his tracks and said, "Wait! I am in a gang. They could kill me if I leave! You just can't drop out of a gang! I mean, I don't want to be in it now at all, but what am I to do?" I said, "Herbie, just leave it in God's hands. He didn't get you saved today to let you be killed. God will take what the enemy meant for evil and turn it to good." He accepted that, smiled, and never expressed another concern about it the rest of the trip.

Herbie got saved that day and went on an immediate mission trip! I so enjoyed watching him in Praise and Worship and clinging onto every word spoken. He even got to share his testimony at a church while he was there. He went from darkness into light and then full speed ahead. You couldn't paint the smile off his face.

After the trip, I saw Herbie a few times at a church we attended in Tulsa. I met his mom and dad who thanked me so much. "I was just the vessel," I explained. His mom brought her hand to her heart and with a twinkle in her eye she said, "This is the answer to my prayers." "I know, I know," I confirmed. Herbie just stood there grinning ear to ear, Bible in his hand, and boasting about all the good things God was doing in his life. It warmed my soul.

Five years passed since that divine appointment with Herb. He was a young man now. One day he was reading the Tulsa news and he came across an article about my daughter, the same one that had the rare blood disease. Some 27 years later, she had been taken by a windstorm in Montana while holding down a trampoline that belonged to her children. She was swooped up off of the ground while on the trampoline and slammed into the ground by the strong winds, leaving her brain dead and on life support. I was traveling back and forth from Tulsa to Montana, staying in hotels to be with my daughter. Herb and his Mom searched for my number after reading the article and contacted me. I was excited to hear from him. He asked if he could stop by. I told him I would love that.

When Herb's car pulled up, I was impressed to see a brand new shiny black car that looked like an Infinity. I was peeking out the window, and out of the car climbed this tall, handsome young man in a three-piece suit. He looked like Wall Street. My doorbell rang, I opened the door, and we embraced. Talk about transformation!

I invited Herb into my home; he had a heartfelt look on his face concerning my daughter. I shared with him that we believed for complete restoration, nothing missing, nothing broken, and that we were standing on God's Word. He smiled that wonderful smile he was blessed with. He began to tell me how much God used me to turn his life around. He and his family were in the process of building their own town in California and a chain of banks. He told me on his desk he kept this picture of him and me in Honduras. He kept it as a reminder of the lady that helped save his life through Jesus and made him the man he is today. It was so good to hear that. He stretched his hand toward me. In it was a check, "My mom wanted you to have this to help with costs. You helped with her son; now she wants to help with your daughter." "Tell your mom I said, "Thank you for the blessing."

We chatted a bit and off he went. I knew God's hand was on everything in his life and mine as well.

Mark 11:24: Therefore I say to you, whatever things you ask when you pray, believe that you receive them, and you will have them.

Thank God for praying mommas. God is good.

Doug Go!

I was accepted and began attending Rhema Bible Training Center in Broken Arrow, Oklahoma in 1996. September of 1997 I had founded a ministry called "The Preaching Workshop." When I first got to Tulsa, I was so excited to hook up my love for the Word and the call on my life. Every time I would get a chance, I would tell people that I was there to go to Rhema. Many times I would get a response back from them saying, "Oh, I went there." Excitedly I would inquire, asking what they were doing now, hoping to hear some fantastic ministerial story of how maybe they became a pastor, missionary, or a praise and worship leader. To my amazement, they would tell me, "Well, I am working at JC Penny's in the men's department," or "I serve tables at a local restaurant." The more and more this happened, the more and more I was dismayed. God, I didn't move all the way to Tulsa to work in a restaurant. What is wrong with this picture! I became grieved in my spirit.

My curiosity rose as I encountered many graduated students. I began to pry a little deeper to find out why they weren't doing anything with their calling. Repeatedly, the replies were similar… "Well, I didn't have pulpit experience, so I was afraid to just go out there and preach." I would pray for them and for God to give them confidence. I also prayed that I would not fall into that same category.

Out of my prayers, God began to give me a vision for a preaching workshop. This would be a ministry where I could put students and graduates in a pulpit to preach. I would schedule them every three to four weeks with four speakers per night to get them experience in the pulpit.

I pioneered The Preaching Workshop. Anyone who wanted to be a part of the workshop must show up to listen to their peers preach. The intercessors would lead prayer, and those called to praise and worship would open our services. It was a wonderful experience to watch the participants go from nervous and timid to bold and powerful ministers. They began flowing in the anointing after getting in the pulpit a few times. Some could barely get a word out their first time in that pulpit, and then within a short period of time, they would have the workshop members on their feet worshipping God. Some of the best preaching I ever heard came right out of that workshop. We experienced huge growth in the hundreds by the end of the first year.

About three years into the pioneering the workshop, it was well known as a place to get seasoned. On one particular night around that third year, a young man only nineteen years old found his way to the workshop. He was a blonde-haired, blue-eyed Cajun boy from Louisiana. He quietly took a seat. We always had new people show up at the workshop. We would go around the room, introduce ourselves, and tell a little about who we are and where we came from.

As everyone took a turn, we came to Dougie. He looked like Dennis the Menace all grown up. There was such innocence about him. He said in his Cajun accent that he just got saved

From the Natural to the Supernatural

a few months ago. He applied and was accepted to Rhema and was called to praise and worship...Screech!!! Hold on a sec, everyone was thinking the same thing. "You are saved less than a year and made it to Rhema?" "Yup," he replied. "OK, you have to tell us your testimony," I said. "That's awesome, but we want to know how you got into Rhema." (Typically you have to be saved at least a year before applying to the school.)

Well, Dougie smiled an innocent smile and began to tell a not so innocent story. He was on drugs, heavy drugs—I believe it was crack cocaine and he was a dealer as well. Doug's life was going nowhere fast, and he was bringing other people down with him. Looking at this boyish young man that had God all over him made it difficult to imagine his story. There was this guy that started witnessing to him and invited him to church. "Well," Doug thought, "I have nothing to lose. Let me see what they have going on there." That night he ended up at the altar giving his life to Christ. He cut himself off from his old friends, broke up with his girlfriend, and followed the Word. Doug's growth was so incredible that someone in his church said to him, "You need to go to Rhema." Dougie just smiled at him, having no idea what Rhema was.

In the days that followed, Doug would keep having this word come up on the inside of him, "Rhema...Rhema...Rhema...you're supposed to go to Rhema." Being young in the Lord, Dougie did not know why this voice kept coming up on the inside of him, but it was the Holy Spirit prompting him.

By the time he was able to reach the next service, he asked this man who mentioned Rhema. "What is Rhema?" "It's a Bible school in Broken Arrow, Oklahoma, founded by

Brother Kenneth Hagin." Oh, OK, Doug had his answer. But he just got saved and didn't know what to think. How could he get accepted into a Bible school so soon after leading the life he led?

The following week again, on the inside, he heard "Rhema" repeatedly. It was like a recording playing over and over in his mind. Being young in the Lord Doug said, "Lord, if You want me to go to this Rhema place, I need a sign."

He headed out for the next church service; he never missed one since he got saved. As he approached the church, he noticed on the movie theater marquis next to the church it said, "Doug Go." He walked around to the other side of the marquis and it said, "Go Doug." "Wow! There is my sign!" He knew it was from God. Sometimes when we are young in the Lord, He will do things like that so you know it is absolutely from Him. Doug took a picture to prove it and showed it to us.

Doug got his sign. He went through the avenues, filled out the application, and got accepted. He had found out about the workshop and had come to get experience doing praise and worship. He had explained to us that he never had done it before. He got a used guitar, without knowing how to play yet, but started self-teaching. He knew, without a doubt, that was what he was supposed to do. Doug heard about the workshop and that it is the place to help people flow in their gifts. It turned out our praise and worship leader for the workshop had just left the week before to go to the next phase of their ministry, so he became our new replacement.

When Dougie started out, the praise and worship was rough, choppy, and hard to follow. I had many members tell me they were struggling with Doug's singing and playing. They wanted me to ask him to step down, but the Lord said no, so I said no. I must say, I think a few members were questioning my credibility in giving Dougie such a position to sharpen his gifts. But God spoke to my spirit and I was to let him learn; after all, that is what the workshop was for.

Within months, Doug had become very good on the guitar. He was a psalmist and his words were simple but powerful. He had the ability to usher us into the presence of God. At times the room would be filled with a glory cloud of the Holy Ghost. Sometimes we would be taken to a whole different direction with his gift. I must say, a lot of members had to eat their words and ask for forgiveness for not trusting God with Doug's call.

Today, Doug travels the world pioneering churches in other countries. Last I heard over forty churches had been started by this young Cajun boy from Louisiana. I am honored for being faithful to God's words spoken to me and for not being influenced by outside groaning.

A simple young man headed down the road of destruction, was now constructing churches, singing, bringing souls into the holy of holies with Holy-Spirit inspired Psalms.

> *1 Corinthians 1:26-28: "For you see your calling, brethren, that not many wise according to the flesh, not many mighty, not many noble, are called. But God has chosen the foolish things of the world to put to shame the wise, and God has chosen the weak things of the world to put to shame the things which are mighty; and the base things of the world and the things which are despised God has chosen, and the things which are not, to bring to nothing the things that are..."*

Jeremiah 1:6-10: *"Ah, Lord God! Behold, I cannot speak, for I am a youth." But the Lord said to me: "Do not say, 'I am a youth,' For you shall go to all to whom I send you, and whatever I command you, you shall speak. Do not be afraid of their faces, For I am with you to deliver you," says the Lord. Then the Lord put forth His hand and touched my mouth, and the Lord said to me: "Behold, I have put My words in your mouth. See, I have this day set you over the nations and over the kingdoms, to root out and to pull down, to destroy and to throw down, to build and to plant."*

What God is saying here is, if you were foolish, I can use you. If you are not mighty, I can use you. If you are not noble, I can use you. If you are weak or base, I can use you. You have got a great résumé! Why? Because He needs the people that were weak to put to shame the mighty! He needs us to confound the wise! How? Don't worry about it. He is going to teach us through His Word. He will put the words of power in our mouths. He will set us over nations and kingdoms! Our Almighty God will make us wise and mighty. We are going to Root Out! Pull Down! Destroy! Throw Down! Build and Plant!

Some of the most broken people are the most fixable and usable in God's eyes. Look at David and the apostle Paul in the Bible. David committed adultery and murdered. Paul killed Christians, yet God used them so mightily. Praise God that at one time you were foolish; it made you a candidate for employment for the Kingdom of the Almighty God.

The Wrong Number or Not?

It was evening, around 10 PM, my time to turn in for the night. I would watch a little television and drift off to sleep, my usual ritual. This particular night was different; the phone rang about 10:15. "Hello." "Hey, is Hosea there?" said the young man on the other end. "No," I answered. "I am sorry. I must have dialed the wrong number. My friend said to call this number and I could get a hold of this dude." "Well," I said. "I am a dudette and you've got the right number." He was confused by my answer.

I went on to tell this young man named Paul that no one calls my number by mistake. He listened intently. I told him God specifically had him call me for a reason, a divine appointment, if you will. "Really, you think so?" he asked. "Absolutely, most definitely," I responded.

I began to tell Paul my personal testimony, then about Jesus. I told him how He knowing what was before Him, sacrificed His own life on the cross for us. I explained that Jesus came to deliver us from sin, sickness, and poverty. "Jesus shed His blood and gave His life so that we may have life and have it more abundantly," I explained. "When we ask Jesus into our hearts He forgives us of our sins, forgets them, takes up residence in our hearts in the Person of the Holy Spirit. We change from the inside out. Our names are then written in the Lamb's Book of Life. We are guaranteed eternal life with Christ, and we will never see hell."

Paul's responses to the knowledge he was receiving were with true amazement. He was taking it all in. "Jesus loves you Paul." Paul was quiet. "The Bible says whoever calls upon the name of the Lord shall be saved. God is no respecter of persons He created me and you and loves both of us to the same degree. He's marked you with a mark with a purpose for you to fulfill. That's why you dialed me tonight. This phone call was no mistake for God, Paul. He doesn't make mistakes." "Would you like to ask Jesus into your heart?" I asked. "Yes, yes I would. How?" Paul asked. "Right now I can pray with you. Your life will never be the same." "OK," he responded. I prayed and he repeated the words asking Jesus to forgive him, save him, and to bring him into the Kingdom of God. Paul's voice quivered as he cried through the whole prayer.

Paul went on to tell me that he and his girlfriend were a mixed couple and they just had a baby. Their families didn't accept them because they were mixed. They felt so much rejection they were out of money and hopeless. "Tonight," he said, "I was going to get drugs from this Hosea guy, then my girlfriend and I were going to overdose and kill ourselves, but instead I got you. I feel so different now on the inside, clean with an inner strength. I don't want to die now. You have no idea how blessed I feel." "God has a plan for you, Paul. That's why you called this dudette," I chuckled. Paul kept repeating, "You just blessed me and changed my life." "Jesus is the one who changed it," I replied. "I was simply the avenue He used."

"I have learned to be obedient and be ready for people who have been in desperate situations, such as yours and mine were." Paul was crying. "I can't wait to tell my girlfriend what you told me about Jesus!" "You might want to pray about getting married and keep it right before God," I instructed. He said they had wanted to get married, but their family was so opposed. "Well, you are a grown man, capable of making your own God-led decisions." "I agree," he said. "Thank you, thank you so much; you have no idea how much you just changed my life. God does love me and is thinking about my family and me. I felt so abandoned and I don't anymore. My girlfriend and I would have been dead if I hadn't called the wrong…or rather, the right number." "God Bless you, Paul and your family," I humbly said. Before we got off the phone I suggested a local church to him and urged him to get a Bible. I told him that Word would be his life book of instruction. He took down all the information and was off on his new journey with God.

Jeremiah 1:5: "Before I formed you in the womb I knew you; Before you were born I sanctified you… [set you apart]"

I laid the phone on the cradle, and my husband looked at me and said, "You don't even have to leave the house." We just smiled, and I thanked the Lord for Paul's salvation and knew they were having a great celebration in Heaven over another soul saved and a double suicide aborted. God is good.

2 Timothy 4:2: Preach the word! Be ready in season and out of season.

Don't miss opportunities that the Lord will put right in front of you. You have within you the power to change lives.

God has ordained you to bring souls out of darkness and into the glorious light. Be willing, obedient, and ready because sometimes you don't even have to leave the house. When you least expect it, God puts someone in your path, and on the inside of you He has equipped you through the Holy Spirit. You will speak supernaturally very powerful words to save a soul and affect this world. Many of us witness to lost souls and we don't close the deal. Why? We don't do it because we are afraid of rejection. I would say in all of my experiences with soul saving, 90 percent say yes the other 10 percent is seed sown. They will later take a walk to the altar or fall to their knees or pray with another asking Jesus into their hearts. Always close the deal. The harvest is ready.

A Yorkie and a Herd of Cattle

Early one morning I woke to the alarming, loud, furious and commanding bark of my four-pound Yorkie named "Bunny." Her bark was much more demanding than I had ever heard before. John yelled to me, "Danielle, you have got to come see this!" I got out of bed to see what all the commotion was about. To my surprise, there was a herd of cattle outside the back door of my house. The cows had escaped their owner's property and headed over to our ranch. Half awake, I noticed that my horses were loose. The cows barreled over our pastures' fencing, setting my horses free. Looking further out, I could see the water spicket was broken off, and water was streaming in the air like a forceful fountain.

Right outside my back door we had installed two-foot high chicken-wire fence to secure our Yorkie's turnout. The cattle were now gathering around the turnout, but no cattle dared to barrel it down with Bunny barking furiously on the other side. She ran back and forth barking her little self silly to keep those cows from coming another inch closer to our house.

Of course being the obsessed "photog" that I am, I ran and grabbed my camera, while John got on the phone with the owner. Hundreds of cattle escaped. I started shooting pictures, being totally amazed at the faces of those cows all lined up around the turnout. They were staring at Bunny dumbfounded. They were way too afraid of our four-pound Yorkie to even think about crossing the borders of the frail chicken-wire fence that encased her. I kept shooting pictures as more and more cattle gathered. All of a sudden, Bunny jumped the turnout and proceeded to round up the cattle and keep them in a tight circle. For a moment I thought she would get trampled, but within a few moments, I realized she had it under control. Those cows were doing exactly what she demanded. This tiny little dog had dominion over hundreds of cattle.

Within an hour, six saddled-up ranch hands appeared to herd up the cattle that left a trail of destruction behind. Bunny kept all those cattle at bay the entire time. This was such a sight! In my life I didn't think I would ever see such a scene as this! Priceless!

After the cows were herded up and headed home, I brought Bunny inside. She was panting heavily and continued to throw out raspy barks toward the back door until all the cows were out of sight. I grabbed a cup of coffee. Climbing back in bed, I downloaded the photos onto my computer. I could not wait to send out the pictures of this major event to my friends and family. I just knew everyone would get a kick out of this!

I clicked the send button, then I began to review the pictures as I sipped away on my cup of Folgers. Staring at every detail in this historic event at the ranch, revelation came upon me. God spoke to my heart, and it continued all day, and I couldn't get the images of Bunny and those cows out of my mind. This teeny tiny little Yorkie kept these massive animals at bay. They could have trampled right over her, and why not? She's just four tiny pounds. Surely she could not take on all those cows, yet none of them came too close. They had torn through forty acres of our horse pastures, ripped out the water spout, trampled down the shrubs, and set our horses free; however, they wouldn't even think about stepping over the tiny little chicken-wire turnout in fear of the wrath of Bunny.

"No one told her she is little," I heard in my spirit. God began to speak to me. "No one told her she wasn't strong. No one told her she couldn't fight those cattle. No one told her she didn't have power." All she knew in her little mind was, "This is my territory, and if you come too close, I am going to kill you!" She didn't see them as giants…she saw them defeated! She held them back with her belief system! She held them back with the knowledge she had acquired as a terrier. Terriers protect, they guard, they fight until they win or die. In her mind she wasn't dying, but those cows were! Bunny's world could have been trampled over and ended that day, but she chose to fight with all the fight within her and her belief system until she achieved the victory!

After realizing what had, in fact, happened that morning, I was a bit ashamed of my belief system and myself. Bunny put me to shame. A four-pound Yorkie had more fight in her than I did, so much fight, she held back an entire herd of cattle. She protected my household and me with her life, just like the Lord protects us.

Who told us that the bills are giants? Who told us that sickness is our giant? Who told us we would be single all our life? Who told us our children wouldn't be saved? Who told us we weren't lovable? Who told us we couldn't have the desire of our hearts? Not God; you can't find any of the above in His Word. Actually, God says the opposite of all those things.

> *1 John 5:4: For whatever is born of God overcomes the world. And this is the victory that has overcome the world—our faith.*

> *Psalm 37:39, 40: But the salvation of the righteous is from the Lord; He is their strength in the time of trouble. And the Lord shall help them and deliver them; He shall deliver them from the wicked, And save them, Because they trust in Him.*

You see, no one ever told Bunny she couldn't beat those cows. She only knew victory and displayed that with every fiber of her being. No defeat! Isn't this how the Lord would have us to be? He tells us the battle is won! We might have to fight off some herds now and then. We will have to take authority over the appearance of defeat! We may have to fight until we are tired and then fight some more! What the Word of God says is: we have the victory! He is in us to fight every battle and to keep it at bay and send it away. Whose voice are we listening to today? Is it the voice of the enemy or the voice of God?

I hope we all can learn a lesson from Bunny and a herd of cattle...

On a Mission

Immediately after I got saved, I was so radically changed that I wanted to tell my best friends, Jerry and Peggy, about Jesus. We used to play in a band together for years. Jerry was our bass player and Peggy, his wife, was a singer. I had grown very close to them over the years; we did a lot of heavy partying together. At the time, I lived an hour and a half away. They were in Long Island and I was in Brooklyn. My first thoughts after I was saved were, "I have to tell Jerry and Peggy about my Jesus so they can have Him too." In my mind, I saw them giving their lives to Christ, getting radically saved and in love with the Lord. I called and Peggy answered. I told her I was coming to visit. She was ecstatic, and she and Jerry made plans for me and my little girl, NayNay, to come the next day. Little did they know that I was on a mission for the Lord.

The whole ride there I kept running different scenarios of what I would say and how they would react. The excitement of getting them saved and on fire filled my soul. I would share my testimony, and I just knew they would receive it. Then they would turn from drugs and the wrong friends and serve God, just like me. The anticipation was overwhelming. My heart began to race as I finally arrived and pulled into their driveway in Mastic, New York.

"Hey! How are you?" they asked as they threw their arms around me pulling me into a giant bear hug. "I am great! Really great!" They invited me in, we walked to the kitchen, and they directed me to the table to have a seat. I pulled out a chair and sat down with both of them. Displayed on the table was my welcoming gift, a bottle of wine and two joints of marijuana. "This is really good weed!" Jerry said and Peggy agreed. "We got blown away when we smoked it." Jerry put his hand forward to grab the joint so he could light it, and I was a little nervous about what to say. I reached out my hand and put it on Jerry's arm before he could get the joint to his mouth and light up. Then these are the words that proceeded out of my mouth: "Jerry, I don't get high on drugs anymore. I get high on Jesus." The silence that followed was the loudest silence I ever heard. I began to tell them my testimony of how I got saved and Jesus healed NayNay. I told them how He delivered me from drugs, cigarettes, hurt, and pain. I boasted of all the wonderful things that Jesus had done for me. I continued telling them that He loves them, too, and wants to be their Lord, too. "He wants to save you and deliver you!" I urged. Of course, in the scenarios that played in my mind, this was the part where they would be touched and want Jesus. Then I would pray with them, and they would get saved. But that is not what took place at all.

Jerry put the joint down and pushed it back. He couldn't light it now, not with the news I just delivered. All of a sudden, the great joy I was welcomed with had shifted to an exchange of a look between them that clearly said I had lost my mind and joined a cult. "No, you guys! It's true Jesus is alive and He wants to be your Lord and Savior!" Waiting for their response felt like an eternity. Jerry looked over at Peggy and said, "Uh, what time were we supposed to be at Tommy and Patti's house?" "About fifteen minutes ago," Peggy spurted out. I was being blown off! Clearly they were lying—we made plans for me to visit and now they were acting as though they had to leave. I just drove an hour and a half to deliver the good news and instead I was being jilted. We even discussed the possibility of me spending the night. Instead I was loading my baby and me back into my car and heading back to Brooklyn. "Jesus, what's the deal? How come they didn't accept You? Why did I drive all the way out here if they were going to reject You?" On my way there it all was going to work out perfectly in my head; instead, I was driving back home with a heavy heart.

I never heard back from Jerry and Peggy. I found out from a close friend that they had divorced about two years later. I thought of them often and how we all lived life dangerously on the edge. I made it through safe with Jesus, but they continued in that lifestyle. I continued to pray for their salvation.

It was about five years later that a R. W. Shambach revival was scheduled in Long Island. I had heard a lot about this minister of God and of all the signs, wonders, and miracles that followed his preaching. When I arrived at the meeting, there was this massive line waiting for seats. Somehow, I was seated in the center of the fifth row. There was just one seat available in the row and an usher escorted me to it. The praise and worship music started in, and I raised my hands and worshipped the Lord. As I stood there, hands lifted up and my face toward Heaven, I heard, "Danielle! Danielle!" I turned to see who was calling me. I looked behind me, and as I was searching with my eyes to find the voice, about three rows behind me I saw Jerry. "I need to talk to you after the meeting!" he exclaimed. "OK, looking forward to it!" I answered. I turned back around and began to praise Jesus for Jerry. It was hard to pay attention. My thoughts were directed on Jerry and what may have happened to bring him to this meeting. My heart smiled.

When the service came to an end, I left my row and searched around for Jerry as I walked toward the door. All of a sudden, there was a tap on my back. I turned. It was Jerry. We embraced. "So, how are you? What's going on with you?" I asked. "Well, I am saved! Yup! I got saved!" He said grinning from ear to ear. "You were the first one to tell me about Jesus, and I thought you lost your mind. Then Peggy and I broke up. I was in such a dark place," he continued. "I didn't want to live anymore. I started to think about what you told us about Jesus. I asked Him to help me, and I made Him the Lord of my life! And it was because you told me about him!" he said with excitement. "Now I am in a Christian band, and I travel all over the world playing for Jesus. I take that big acoustic bass you gave me everywhere and give my testimony. I tell how you came and told me about Jesus. I am saved because of you!" "Jerry, I am so happy for you! I have been praying for you for years." We chatted a bit and then we departed.

I climbed in to my car and was in complete and utter amazement at God's faithfulness to His Word. He hears our prayers and answers them. His words did not return void! Those words the Lord had me speak were seared into Jerry's heart and waiting for the perfect moment to perform what they were meant for. My heart was warmed, and I smiled all the way home…I'm smiling right now as I write about it. God is good all the time.

Isaiah 55:11: So shall My word be that goes forth from My mouth; It shall not return to Me void, but it shall accomplish what I please, And it shall prosper in the thing for which I sent it.

When we are obedient to witness, we may not see a result at that very moment. We must never forget that God's Word has power, and when it is planted in someone's heart, one day it will sprout up. They will make a choice whether to accept it and nurture it until it grows to maturity. So don't be discouraged if you don't get an immediate result after witnessing. Sometimes we just have to be obedient to sow the Word, and some other way it will blossom. Always try to seal the deal. Never get discouraged if you can't at that moment. It's going to be in God's timing, so never question it.

The Girl in the Hotel

On a ten-day mission trip to Haiti, we were scheduled morning meetings inside the stadium and evening meetings out on the field. We stayed in a hotel in the middle of one of Haiti's poorest cities. I was on a wing of the hotel with three other ministers, and I was the only female minister on that particular trip.

The hotel was large and probably conceived as a rich man's place to dwell, but the room I was in was full of Geckos that would run across my face and body at night. When I showered, I noticed the water was brown, and when I finished my shower, a mud-like substance would lie on the top on the tub floor. We were instructed not to drink the water while in Haiti, but I made the mistake of running my toothbrush under the water faucet while brushing my teeth.

It seemed like every day I would see this young lady at the hotel, sometimes at the front desk, sometimes in the café area and in the halls. She was an attractive girl, usually in a miniskirt or shorts. I felt drawn to her and knew on the inside of me that God was preparing me to witness to her. I was waiting for an appropriate time to present itself. Whenever I would see this young lady, I would pray, "Lord, if you want me to tell her about You, please open the door."

It was the evening of the third day when I had become very sick to my stomach, a parasitic infection, no doubt, from brushing my teeth with the water. After being up all night doubled over in pain and making many trips to the bathroom, we all agreed I should stay back that day and overcome this physical challenge. We prayed for healing, and the men went off without me.

Around noon I started to have an appetite and decided to make my way to the café. I would just order some plain white rice, a nice safe source of substance. I threw on some jeans, a shirt, and flip-flops and queasily made my way through the hotel to the outside café. I felt woozy and dizzy from my lack of sleep and dehydration from the night before. I was pale and gray. I was not in any way interested in having anyone see me or talk with me. I just wanted rice and my bed.

I ordered my rice and clung onto my stool. All of a sudden, I noticed the young lady walking toward the café. Oh, Lord, I thought, not today. I just want to go lie down. Not surprisingly, she took the seat right next to mine. There was no one behind the counter; they were off making my rice. Only one person worked in the café, who took your order, cooked your food, and served it to you, so she was in for a wait.

"Hello," I introduced myself. "Hello," she replied with a bit of an accent. "I have seen you around the hotel for a couple of days," I added. "I have seen you as well," she agreed. I will call her "Noelle" because the nature of where this story will go requires that I need to protect my new friend. Noelle told me she was from Haiti and was going to College in Canada. She was returning to see her mom who was high in the government in Haiti. We chatted, and I asked her how her visit with her mom was going. I was surprised to hear she hadn't even seen her yet, and her mom didn't even know she was there. I was chronicling in my mind the last three days and how it seemed like Noelle had never left the hotel. I would see her during my times of comings and goings. I pushed those thoughts aside and started my internal conversation with the Lord, "OK, Lord, you put this girl on my heart. Now open the door and speak your words through me." Even though I just wanted to lie down, I was assigned to a mission, so I let the spiritual adrenaline kick in. "Noelle, would you like to have lunch together?" I asked. "Yes, that would be nice," she accepted. We moved to a small round table located outside, she ordered, and we began to chat. Noelle seemed to be happy to have someone to connect with. "So, what brings you to Haiti?" she inquired. Here was my open door and my shift in the spirit. "Well, we are here doing a ten-day crusade in the football stadium, morning and evening meetings." Noelle looked at me curiously and asked me what a crusade was. I explained that we had come from the United States to preach the gospel of Jesus Christ to the Haitian people. I explained that we had come to bring hope, encouragement, salvation, miracles, and healing. "You really believe that?" she asked. "Absolutely!" I responded. "Do you want to know what Jesus did for you?" I asked. "Yes, I would like to know," Noelle replied as she leaned in to hear all about my Jesus. I told her of how God sent His only Son as a sacrifice to deliver us from sin, sickness, and evil. Noelle was now listening intently. I told her of how He gave His life through the crucifixion because of His love for us. He rose again and lives, and we can ask Him into our hearts. Then immediately He enters in through the person of the Holy Spirit. He will never leave us or forsake us, because

He takes up residency on the inside of us. I gave Noelle my personal testimony and God pricked her in her heart.

I didn't even have to offer salvation to her; she asked me, "How can I have Jesus? Where do I go to get Him?" I answered, "You don't have to go anywhere. I can pray with you right now and He will come in to your heart." "Yes, let's pray!" Noelle responded. I took her hand and told her to repeat after me. "Dear Jesus, I believe You are the Son of God. I believe that You gave your life on the cross so that I would be forgiven of my sins. Forgive me now. Come into my heart and be my Lord and Savior." Tears streamed down Noelle's cheeks, and her lips quivered as we prayed. I threw my arms around her and hugged her while she wept. "I feel Him, I feel Him on the inside of me," she mumbled almost unable to speak. I reassured her that He would always be with her no matter what. I ate lunch with my newly saved friend as she went on to talk about what she was experiencing on the inside. "I feel like I want to love everyone," Noelle exclaimed. "Yup, that's what Jesus does to us," I confirmed. "Hey, Noelle, would you like to come to the crusade tonight and sit with me on the platform?" I asked. "Can I? Really?" "Yes, of course." We ate our lunch as Noelle's name was being written into the Lamb's Book of Life. The angels held a big party in heaven over Noelle's salvation. I was healed of the stomach problem immediately, but what was yet to come was shocking.

We were to meet and leave the hotel for the stadium around 6:00 PM. At 5:00 PM there was a knock on my door. It was Stan, one of my fellow ministers I traveled with. Standing beside Stan was Noelle. They looked very serious. "What's up guys?" I asked. They looked like they had swallowed a frog. In my mind I was thinking maybe I was going to prison for introducing Noelle to Jesus. "We have a problem," Stan said.

From the Natural to the Supernatural

I invited them in and we all took a seat on the bed. "Noelle, tell her," Stan encouraged, and Noelle began to cry. "I was flown here by a very dangerous cocaine dealer. I entered the country of Haiti with several pounds of cocaine on a belt around my waist. (Now this was before "9-11" and security wasn't as tight as it is today). "I am supposed to meet this man, deliver the cocaine, and receive the money for it. I took the offer because it meant a free trip to see my family," she explained. Now in tears she said, "I have Jesus in my heart now and I don't want to do it. If I don't, they will kill me! I don't know what to do! They were supposed to pick it up already and they kept postponing. That is why I am still in this hotel," she cried. "No, Noelle, you are still here because of Jesus. He didn't allow you to be saved to let you be killed. His Word says, no weapon formed against you shall prosper." "Well, what do I do?" she asked. "You said your mom is high in the government, right? Well, call her, tell her what has happened, and she will get you protected." I suggested. "No, she will kill me if she knows!" she insisted. "Noelle, she's your mom. She will protect you. That is a mother's first instinct. Then she will kill you later," I chuckled. That brought a smile to Noelle's face. "But I can't tell her," she said. "Well, let's just pray," I said. Stan, Noelle, and I lifted the situation up to Jesus and put it in His hands. Noelle was calmer after that; I could see her little mind going at a thousand miles a minute. We agreed that we were going to go to the crusade and just enjoy God for the evening.

When Stan and Noelle left the room, I dropped to my knees. "Lord, now I know why You held me back here at the hotel today. You love Noelle. You have drawn her to You. Please keep her protected and safe." If I had not stayed back that day, Noelle would be pulling off a major drug deal and still be in danger of her life. God never ceases to amaze me at the orchestration of His plans. He took what the devil meant for evil (the stomach ailment) and used it for good. I knelt there just awestruck at the whole day. Now it was off to the crusade to witness more salvations, healing and miracles.

Noelle met us in the lobby. She had a cute little suit on. When I say "little" I mean the skirt was a mini, but it was all she had. We loaded into the jeep, and we were off to the next episode of the day. When we arrived at the stadium, it was already packed body to body with the Haitian people. Security made a blocked aisle to get us to the platform. Witnessing the look on Noelle's face was priceless. We were seated in the front row, on the platform, with many visiting ministers from Haiti. There were about 40,000 people that particular night. Praise and worship started, and Noelle got right into it, praising God for her salvation. When we were seated, I kept noticing Noelle adjusting her skirt. She was trying to pull it down in an attempt to stretch the fabric to make it a few inches longer, but to no avail. The skirt length was convicting Noelle on and off through the service. I didn't care about it. I was just glad to have her there. Again, I glanced over at her and this time tears were flowing down her face. "What's wrong, Noelle?" I inquired. "I am just realizing how much God loves me. I get saved today, and tonight I am sitting here in such an honorable place. What have I done to deserve this?" "You became a daughter of the King, and now you are a princess. Don't question it—just enjoy it." I put my arm around her shoulder and gave her a squeeze.

The crusade was powerful that night as the anointing on God's Word performed supernatural healings, miracles, salvation, and deliverance from witchcraft. Noelle's eyes were as wide as a Frisbee as she took in God's Word in action.

Thousands came to the altar for each of their individual needs to be met. Folks were coming out of wheelchairs and off crutches. Evil spirits were coming out of the demon possessed as they gave their lives to Christ.

I thought, "Could anyone even imagine getting saved and a few hours later becoming a witness to all of this?" This was salvation overload! Nevertheless, it was just the way God had it to be for Noelle.

We grabbed a bite to eat after the crusade and headed for the hotel. I said goodnight to Noelle, and we gave each other a hug. I climbed into bed and couldn't wait to see my little friend the next day. "God bless her and keep her" were my prayers before drifting off into a much-needed sleep. Little did I know that would be the last time I would see Noelle.

I was awakened in the morning by the phone ringing in my hotel room. I was a little groggy when I answered. A woman was on the other end of the line. "Hello, is this Danielle?" the voice asked. "Yes, it is," I said. "Hi, Danielle, this is Melia, Noelle's mother." My heart skipped a beat, and I had a surge of my nerves streamline through my body. "What now," I thought. Was I in trouble? She continued, "I don't know what you did to my daughter, but I want to thank you." Oh, thank God, I thought she was going to ask me to undo Noelle's salvation, which is impossible. "Well, I didn't do anything. God did it. I just was the messenger," I replied. Melia continued, "Thank you so much. I wanted to let you know, I am picking her up and getting her into hiding. I also want to let you know how grateful we are." "I understand. I have two daughters as well, and moms are protectors. She's in God's hands now, and He will protect her. Thank you for calling, and tell her I love her."

That was it. Noelle was out of my life as fast as she came in. All within less than twenty-four hours, wow! It's comforting to know Jesus is in her life now and saved her from a potentially life-threatening situation. God performed so many miracles on that crusade. I experienced the power of God in every situation. In my mind, all the lives that would be touched would be for those who showed up at the crusade, but I was wrong. Hanging back from a stomach ailment caused one of the greatest miracles ever. The miracle of salvation…

Jeremiah 29:11: For I know the thoughts that I think toward you, says the Lord, thoughts of peace and not of evil, to give you a future and a hope.

A Journey to Hell

I attended Rhema Bible Training Center where I met many, many students with testimonies that were powerful, but one student in particular stands out in my mind. It was a man named "Dale." Dale was tall and rugged looking. When he walked in the room, he demanded attention, but he wasn't even aware of it. I had the honor of getting to know him as my friend and found him to be a gentle, kind, loving man who would give you the shirt off his back.

One day Dale and I were chatting and I asked him what his story was. I was blown away at the testimony he proceeded to tell. When he was a young boy, he was diagnosed with polio. It had become so severe that by the time he was a teenager he was placed in an iron lung to keep him alive. No device is more related to polio than the iron lung. Physicians found that patients with acute early stages of polio had muscle groups in the chest that paralyzed the muscles, making it very difficult to breathe. The poliovirus was characterized by fever, motor paralysis, and atrophy of skeletal muscles often with permanent disability and deformity. The disease-transferring agent, poliovirus, is spread mostly through contact by mouth with an already infected person. For those infected whose bodies do not successfully combat the poliovirus, the outcome is horrific. In these cases, the sufferers typically experience neck and back stiffness and muscle weakness, often leaving the patient paralyzed and deformed. Dale was robbed of a normal childhood in exchange for a life of pain and suffering. He was a prisoner to the iron lung with no quality of life—just pain. Wow! And I thought I had a rough childhood.

Now I am looking at a man before me who looks completely whole, straight, and healthy. "So what happened?" I asked. He continued to tell me that he wasn't saved and was close to death. One day his spirit left his body. He was traveling down this cylinder at a fast speed. As he progressed in his journey downward, the cylinder began to get hot, red hot! Dale said he put out his arms and legs against the cylinder so as not to go any farther. When he came to a halt, he saw hell. He went on to tell me that there was a sea of fire, and the inhabitants were screaming and clawing their own flesh from the scorching burn of their skin. Dale saw people he knew down there, which was terrifying. He said to me, "You know, Danielle, how someone tells another person they are going to hell without Jesus, and they say, 'Oh, well, that's OK—all my friends will be there.' Well, they are in so much pain down there, that they don't care if you are there or not. There is no partying in hell. It is eternal torture and torment."

> *Matthew 8:12: "But the sons of the kingdom will be cast out into outer darkness. There will be weeping and gnashing of teeth."*

"So what did you do, Dale?" I asked. "I started screaming, 'Oh Jesus! Oh Jesus!'" he said. "Then the more I said it, the farther up the cylinder I went," he continued. "As I started back up, a huge hand came down. I grabbed onto it and it pulled me up to my room and back to my body." Dale said he was trembling after he returned. Then right there in his iron lung, he asked Jesus into his heart. Immediately Dale was saved, healed, and all polio and its symptoms were gone! He dedicated his life to serving God from that day forward.

What a testimony! I was so awed at his story I just had to write it. We all have testimonies to share, so we should share them. There is power in our testimonies that give glory to God. When I first got saved, all I had was my testimony that I shared and brought others to salvation.

Revelation 12:11: And they overcame him by the blood of the Lamb and by the word of their testimony,

Dale had a powerful testimony that he shared with many and touched a lot of lives by causing them to make decisions for Christ.

Salvation Vacation

It had been over twenty years since I had seen my aunt Elsie, uncle Joe, my cousin Dennis, his wife Terri, and their son, Aaron. Now all of them had retired to Melbourne, Florida. My two sisters and their families were residing there as well. Most of them bought their retirement homes in the same subdivision. You could literally walk across the street or go out the back door and be at one of their houses.

I had been in contact with my cousins, and we were excited to re-connect as we planned for me to come for a vacation. I made my flight plans, landed in Tampa, and rented a car. I would visit with my mom and brother first. Mom lived on the other side of the state, and I hadn't seen her in quite a while because of work, and she doesn't fly. She barely leaves the house for that matter. My mom is one of the nicest, kindest persons I have ever known. We had a wonderful visit, and after three days, I packed up the car and headed for Melbourne, a three-hour drive.

I was excited to see my aunt, uncle, and cousins, but I must admit, I had an agenda. Throughout my life, I prayed for their salvation. We were raised in a very "religious and legalistic" traditional church. We were taught about Jesus, but never had a personal relationship. We learned He was the Son of God, was crucified and rose again, but it ended there. We didn't know or learn about the fact that His blood was shed for us, so we could be redeemed, saved, and Spirit filled. Jesus was this distant and mysterious character that common people like myself would never be worthy of. After finding Jesus on my own, all of that changed and I dedicated my life to sharing His message.

On my trip there I prayed that the Lord would open the door for me to share Him with my unsaved family. They are great people. My aunt said the rosary every day several times a day. When my cousin Dennis was a baby, he had a large tumor in his abdomen that should have killed him. My aunt pleaded with God that if He would spare her son, she would pray the rosary every day for the rest of her life. She had lived up to that commitment, and I believe God honored it. Aunt Elsie was an intercessor. She did it the only way she knew how, and that was with the rosary beads.

My family being all-Italian, a feast was prepared before my arrival. I always look forward to that part of Italian family gatherings. I pulled in the driveway, and my cousin Dennis and his wife greeted me with open arms. We stood back and looked at each other and decided we looked the same except a little older. I met Aaron, their son, who had grown up to be a nice, good-looking young man now in college. Terri led me to my room, and I parked my suitcase. In the meantime, the internal conversation with God, "Lord, open the door and give me the words to say to glorify You and that they would be saved." Internal conversations with God have become a way of life for me.

Dennis had whipped up some of his delicious specialties: stuffed mushrooms, barbecued chicken and ribs, a plate of fresh veggies. We sat in the screened-in porch that had an in-ground pool. We were eating and gabbing along, catching up on the last twenty years, and laughing so hard tears streamed down our faces. My aunt Elsie and Uncle Joe joined us, and they were just ecstatic to see me. Aunt Elsie hadn't seemed to change a bit, 84 years old and still looked like she was in her sixties, but Uncle Joe had grown frail and a little unstable in his gait. Nevertheless, we were together again and it was great! We nibbled away and enjoyed each other's company. I was pleased there wasn't any awkwardness after so many years apart. We picked up right where we left off. Uncle Joe kept hugging me and looking at me like he was beholding me. He didn't say much, but he was just so happy to see me again.

After we ate and chatted a bit, it was time to take the tour of all my relatives' houses in the neighborhood. First on the list were Aunt Elsie and Uncle Joe's home. Then it was off to my sisters, and continuing on my tour to my cousin Debbie's home. Some of the houses looked just alike, and they all had in-ground pools that were screened in with beautiful patios, plants, and furniture. "What a beautiful place to retire," I thought.

Well, it was getting late and it was back to Dennis and Terri's for the next presentation and partaking of delicious food. Aaron had to leave for a few hours, so after dinner it was just the three of us. I was still waiting for an opportunity to present itself to tell them about Jesus but nothing yet. After dinner and the dishes were done, Dennis asked if I would like to see a movie. I thought it sounded like a great idea, so we got in our jammies and settled in on the couches—Dennis, Terrie and I. We watched a comedy and laughed throughout the film, but in my spirit, I was conversing with God about their salvation.

The movie ended and we started to talk. They started asking me questions about the Christ-centered equine therapeutic riding ranch I pioneered in 2006. It was for abused and neglected horses and challenged youth. They were very intrigued at the concept and wanted to know more. I shared with them how much the kids' lives changed at the ranch as well as the horses'. I gave all the glory to God, which led to the part about Jesus. I shared how Jesus touched the hearts of the youth, parents, and volunteers. They listened intently as I spoke of the things of God and how Jesus was more than someone we learned about. I explained He is alive and wants a personal relationship with us. I shared testimony after testimony. I could see in their faces and body language they were taking it all in, so I popped the question. "Would you like to make Jesus your Lord and Savior and have a personal relationship with Him? We can pray a prayer right now and you can be saved," I explained. "Yes, we would," they replied. My spiritual adrenaline was pumping! We held each others hands as they repeated after me the salvation prayer, bringing them into the Kingdom and making them joint heirs with Christ! It was just precious. I always desired for my whole family to be saved. It was very quiet after we finished praying. God was present, and we could all feel Him right there in the midst of us. No one said a word.

After the silence broke, I explained how it is important to read the Bible. "It is our instruction book. It tells us who we are in Him and is full of God's promises," I explained. We talked about their salvation being eternal and that they would never see hell. They took it all in. It was getting late and we all agreed we needed to get some sleep, so we retired for the night. I fell asleep thanking God for His goodness and for sacrificing His Son Jesus so that we could be saved.

I woke the next morning to the smell of a fresh breakfast being made. Dennis was in the kitchen flipping pancakes. On the table was a mug waiting for me with a pot of fresh coffee. I don't know when the last time had been that I had such a great breakfast prepared for me. Dennis, Terri, and I sat at the table and blessed the food and began to eat. Then with a serious tone to her voice, Terri said to me, "Look, I don't understand what happened last night, but we do things as a family, and if Dennis and I are saved, then you need to get our son Aaron saved." I about choked on my coffee. "I can try to do that," I replied. "Good, he's in his room," Terri answered as she looked toward Aaron's bedroom door and nodded. OK then. I took a sip of my coffee, grabbed my Bible, and was on my way to Aaron's room to do an on-the-spot salvation plea, with no leading of the Spirit right at that moment. Knock, knock, knock on the door. "Who is it?" Aaron asked, "It's Aunt Danielle." "Come in," he said. I opened the door. Aaron was sitting at his desk working on the computer and finishing up his thesis. "You got a minute? I have something I want to share with you," I said nervously. "Give me fifteen minutes, Aunt Danielle." "OK, great! Let me know when you are ready."

It was more like a half an hour, but it felt like an eternity to me. Dennis and Terri were sitting at the table in desperation for their son's salvation. I was not feeling anointed at the moment, and I will admit a little fear started to set in as I sat there, Bible in hand. Finally, I started rebuking the spirit of fear, binding and loosing, and prepared to go in on a cold call. "Be ready in season and out of season," I repeated in my mind.

"OK, Aunt Danielle, I'm ready," Aaron called from his room. Dennis and Terri looked at me as if to say, "Good luck." I took a seat on Aaron's bed. He was sitting backwards in his computer chair looking right at me. "Well, Aaron, I am here to tell you about something that took place with your mom and dad last night. You see we talked about Jesus and why He came, how He gave His life and shed His blood for us, so we may be forgiven of our sins. He wants a personal relationship with us, so your parents asked Jesus into their hearts last night and made Him their Lord and Savior." Aaron listened intently. I couldn't tell if he was taking me seriously or if he was just being polite.

I opened up the Bible and shared some scriptures with him about Jesus explaining that He was the Way to saving our souls. Throughout my babbling, he would nod to affirm me. "So, Aaron," I continued, "this morning your mom and dad came to me and told me that you all do things as a family unit, so I am here to ask you a question." "OK," Aaron replied. "Would you like to ask Jesus into your heart to be your Lord and Savior just like your parents did last night?" I said, as my heart raced. "Yeah, I would," he replied. Wow! I thought on the inside, "I had no idea that he would receive this so well!" I reached out my hand. He took it into his and together we prayed and Aaron got saved! Dennis and Terrie were elated! Their household was now saved. My sister Roseanne walked over to have coffee, and Dennis announced, "Roseanne, me, Terri, and Aaron got saved!" "Praise the Lord! That's wonderful!" she exclaimed. "Let's have a water baptism in your pool tonight!" she suggested. She explained to them what the water baptism meant and represented. So that night, my brother-in-law, Frankie, and I baptized Dennis, Terri, and Aaron with my two sisters and their husbands present. It was a beautiful thing. Dennis was so cute when he said, "I got saved and baptized in my own pool, all within twenty four hours. I never had to leave the house!" he proclaimed with a big smile. "Danielle, you have to get my mother and father saved too," he said. "Oh Lord," I thought, "Dennis wants to know his whole family is covered! That's awesome!" But how would the Lord have me bring my aunt and uncle to Jesus? They came from a very devout religious background. Wait a minute, I was from the same devout religious background as they were, and I got saved! However, I had been attending non-denominational churches since I got saved. "I had been dropping seeds to my aunt and uncle since I arrived," I thought to myself. Then the lies entered into my mind, "Yeah, but they are in their eighties. You were twenty-three, they are set in their ways." Then the voice of reason, called the Holy Spirit, would give a rebuttal…"All things are possible to those who love Christ Jesus; My word shall not return to me void." This was a desire I had since the day I got saved…for all of my family to get saved.

On Sunday, Dennis, Terrie, Aaron, and my family went to a church, the pastor of which was a friend of mine. Everyone enjoyed the service and met the pastor. We invited him and his wife over the next day for dinner. I had a motive, and that was having pastor get my Aunt Elsie and Uncle Joe saved—genius!

We ate dinner and then went over to my aunt and uncle's house. We chatted a bit and my aunt asked him to bless her house. "Cool," I thought. "Maybe he will do a salvation invitation, too, and they would accept Jesus." We walked over to Aunt Elsie's. We all held hands. Aunt Elsie, Uncle Joe, Dennis, Terri, Aaron, my sister Roseanne, her husband Frank, my sister Laureen, and her husband Roy. The pastor prayed a blessing over the house, which was so wonderful, but nothing about salvation. "Amen," everyone repeated after the prayer and then they released each other's hands. "Wait a minute!" I blurted out. "I don't think we are done. Everyone hold hands again!" I knew everyone there was aware of what was coming next, because they know me…that is, everyone but Aunt Elsie and Uncle Joe. We all clasped hands, then the words came out of my mouth, but they were not from me. The words came from God. "I know some of us here know Jesus as our Lord and Savior and some of us know about Him but haven't made Him Lord of our lives by asking Him into our hearts. So if you would like to ask Him into your heart right now, I am going to ask you to pray this prayer with me." Everyone joined in as my aunt and uncle prayed, "Dear Jesus, I believe You are the Son of God. I believe You died on the cross for me. Forgive me for my sins. Come into my heart and be my Lord and Savior. In Jesus name I ask. Amen." It was sealed! My aunt and uncle were saved!

After most everyone left, I sat on the couch with my frail Uncle Joe. He was so chatty! "Danielle, where did you learn to pray like that?" he blurted. "I have never heard anyone pray like that! I felt it, like a power came inside of me!" he continued. "Yes, Uncle Joe, that feeling was the Holy Spirit taking up residency on the inside of you. You belong to God now. You will never see hell." His eyes were wide and he was so energized. "You are an angel, and you should go pray all over the world!" he exclaimed. "No, Uncle Joe, I am not an angel. I am just a believer, a vessel that God works through. God gave those words power to save you." Aunt Elsie was standing there watching and listening, then she said, "I haven't heard him talk this much in years. This is amazing!" "It's the power of God, Aunt Elsie, Uncle Joe is experiencing the power of God." Uncle Joe's facial expression was priceless.

We all went back to our homes. It was late and an eventful night. I was leaving in two days. I went shopping with the family and bought Bibles for everyone. Leaving was difficult, but I knew they were in good hands with Jesus.

I am happy to report that they joined a good nondenominational church in their town. They attend church every week, including my Aunt Elsie. I talked with her on the phone, and she was excited about the church. "We sing and worship, and then the pastor teaches us things from the Bible. It makes you understand God and His Word. I never learned stuff like this in my church." "I know, Aunt Elsie. God is good." "Yes, He is." "Thank you so much. Because of you, we are all serving God and going to church." I knew it was because of my prayers and desires.

> *Acts 16:31: So they said, "Believe on the Lord Jesus Christ, and you will be saved, you and your household."*

A few months later, my Uncle Joe went home to be with the Lord. My aunt told me she made him breakfast as she always did. One morning when she called him to come eat, he didn't come. After going to his room to check on him, he was sitting on the side of the bed looking upward (toward heaven no doubt). He wouldn't respond, just stared. Uncle Joe lived a few more weeks before he went home to be with the Lord. He is now spending eternity with his Heavenly Father. His salvation came right on time, and he is in our future.

You may desire for a family member or members to be saved today. Pray and ask God for them. It is His desire as well. When we pray and believe, we set God into action on our behalf. Sometimes God uses us and sometimes He uses other channels. I have had the honor of praying with many of my family members, even my own mother. Sometimes with family they will receive from you and sometimes it has to come from another source. Just stay faithful that He is able to perform it…and, just in case, be ready in season and out of season.

> *2 Timothy 4:2: Preach the word! Be ready in season and out of season. Convince, rebuke, exhort, with all longsuffering and teaching.*

The Blind Man

I was on a mission trip in Haiti. The stadium was over packed with 40,000 people or more. We would be there ten days with meetings in the morning inside the stadium and evening meetings outside on the field. God had done many amazing things, but it was the third evening that left one of the largest impressions on me, one I would never forget.

The field was packed tight; the crowd was body to body. The Haitian people had their hopes high. I could literally feel the pull of the people expecting a move of God. I prayed for God to deliver them and answer their prayers. I only had about fifteen minutes to speak before the main speaker. Basically, I was a warm-up speaker that night, but the fifteen minutes were powerful. Not only did the people in the crowd get revelation from the anointed words of God, but the guest pastors did as well.

My short teaching was from a sermon I wrote called "What You Say, Is What You Get." The crowd was roused up and praised God with the words that enlightened their hearts. I spoke on our words and that they have creative power, explaining that we need to make sure our words line up with God's Word. I gave them examples of how the Word says we are not poor, but we are rich. We are not sick, but we are healed. We are not given a spirit of fear, but power, love, and a sound mind. I quickly brought them through the different ways Jesus healed. He spoke a word, and they were healed. He touched them, and they were healed. Their faith made them whole. I taught about the blind man who was given his sight and those with unclean spirits that were cast out of them. I could feel the crowd pulling for more.

My morning meeting was delivered with the anointing of God. The people responded so well and the altar call included almost the entire crowd of people. Of about five hundred, all but five people responded. People were getting saved, healed, and delivered from demonic strongholds and witchcraft. "Powerful!" would sum up that meeting in one word. I was so thrilled for the Haitian people to get answers to their prayers!

That evening I could sense the people were understanding the message and pulling on me. Then all of a sudden I felt a hand on my shoulder. It was my fellow minister telling me my time was up. It was right smack dab in the middle of my sentence. The people and the fellow ministers were not happy about it. I turned around and took a seat. It was hardly fifteen minutes. Inside the internal conversation was going, "Why God? Why would he do something like this?" I then heard on the inside, "It's not him, it's the enemy." Those present were getting revelation knowledge and the devil didn't like it. I just had to trust God that He got over to them what they needed to receive.

When the preaching was over, he prayed for people, and I prayed with him, as he did the altar call. We finally left the platform and a chunk of the crowd started to hurl my way. Security was trying to hold them back, but several determined people made their way to me. A woman and a blind man came to me. She spoke English. She began to tell me that he was fifty-three years old and had been blind from birth. As I looked at the man, I noticed a milky white covering over his eyes. His eyes went in two different directions. "He wants to see!" she said. I said a short internal prayer, "Not me, but You, Lord, that this man would testify of what You have done." I told her to ask the man if he believed Jesus would heal him. He answered, "Yes." "Tell him to close his eyes," I instructed her. When he closed his eyes, I put my thumbs on them and then I said, "Eyes be opened in the name of Jesus." When I removed my thumbs, I noticed most of the milky substance was gone. He was staring right at me. He told the woman he could see something. "Tell him to close his eyes again," I said. She instructed him and again I put my thumbs on his eyes. "Eyes be opened and completely restored," I prayed. This time his eyes were clear and his eyes lined up. He stared at me like no one has ever done before. He would blink and then say something over and over. "He is saying, 'You are an angel, you are an angel,'" she said. "No, tell him I am just a vessel that God used to give him his sight. It's God's supernatural ability working through me. Tell him only God can do this for him," I said.

I will never forget those eyes and the look on that man's face. It stays permanently embedded in my mind.

> *Matthew 9:27-30: When Jesus departed from there two blind men followed Him, crying out and saying, "Son of David, have mercy on us!" And when He had come into the house, the blind men came to Him. And Jesus said to them, "Do you believe that I am able to do this?" They said*

> to Him, "Yes, Lord." Then He touched their eyes, saying, "According to your faith let it be to you." And their eyes were opened.

Their miracle depended on their faith. They believed Jesus was able to give them their sight. We have been ordained to do the works that Jesus did in all humility. The glory goes to God.

> Luke 4:18: The Spirit of the Lord is upon Me. To preach the gospel to the poor; He has sent Me to heal the brokenhearted, To proclaim liberty to the captives And recovery of sight to the blind, To set at liberty those who are oppressed.

This man had received a precious gift that night. When God is trying to get something to you, He can pick you out of a million people just to get you! He knows our hearts. He knows our desires. He knows our needs. We just need to believe He is able and put our faith into action. This blind man put his faith into action by pushing through the crowd and bringing an interpreter along with him. He believed that if he could get to me, for me to pray for him, he would receive his sight through Jesus. He stood body to body, for hours waiting for his moment. He was not going to let it pass by. He fought obstacles, such as the crowd and security, to get his miracle! He came to get something from God, and he wasn't going home without it!

Faith and determination got him his sight. He fought for it, and no one was going to stop him. How determined are we? Do you stay focused on the prize? Or do you give up when there are obstacles in the way? Do you push through to the finish line or throw the towel in? Do you give up because it just seems to be too hard? Or it takes too long? Don't give up and never give in! Keep your eye on the prize and make your way to the finish line. Grab on to your dream. It already belongs to you. You just have to take it, no matter what may try to stand in your way. Hold fast to your faith.

An Hour to Live

I was getting ready to run errands when I received a call from my friend Sharon. She was at the hospital with her mom. "Danielle, they have given my mother an hour to live. Get here right away!" she said with urgency in her voice. Sharon was a prayer warrior. We prayed together many times, and God would show up. We would hold prayer meetings at her house, and people would end up all over the floor, slain in the Spirit and delivered from whatever they came to get delivered from. Sharon's mom, Virginia, had become very dear to me. She was my "stand in" grandma. I loved her. She was a tiny gray-haired lady with piercing blue eyes and a gigantic heart. She loved Jesus—there was no doubt about that.

Virginia had grown fragile over a year's time and was barely eating. I think it was emotional more than physical, but the emotions were taking a toll on her health. She seemed to lose her zest for life. She had moved in with Sharon because she could no longer live on her own. Her frame became very frail and weak. I believe she was giving up on life because of some discord between family members.

When I got the call, I scurried to my car and headed toward the hospital to be by Sharon's side. I only hoped

Virginia would live until I arrived. I searched for a parking space. There was construction all around the hospital and I knew every moment was vital for me to reach Virginia's room. I was praying in the Spirit the whole time, feverently! Finally, I found a parking space two blocks from the hospital! I sprinted all the way up the very steep hill that led to the entrance. Now I was in a full sweat as I pushed the elevator button. "Please, Lord, let Virginia be alive when I get there," I prayed.

Finally, I approached her room and walked in. I saw Sharon and Len facing Virginia on the right side of her bed so they were able to see me when I entered. Len looked up at me. His face was full of gloom. I glanced at Sharon. I could tell she was just glad to see me. As I passed the curtain that divided Virginia from her roommate, I stood on the other side of the bed facing Len and Sharon. I was ready to hook up in prayer with my prayer warrior friend. But I had to be hooked up with those who believed, and I wasn't so sure about Len. Looking at the two of them I said, "Anyone in unbelief must leave the room." I knew Sharon would stand with me, but to my amazement, I saw belief hop over on to Len.

Looking down at Virginia, she was skin on bones. Her breath was rapid and short, and she lay unconscious. Her bony chest was revealing the difficulty of her breathing. It was quite visible that within minutes, she was ready to pass. I began praying in the Spirit with Sharon and Len. The anointing kicked in and it was powerful! We prayed and bound and rebuked the spirit of death. We bound and loosed, agreeing together for her life.

After about ten minutes of pressing in, Virginia opened her eyes. She looked at me and asked if she could have a sip of Pepsi. "Someone get her a Pepsi!" I boasted. Sharon happened to have a Pepsi in the room and ice. She popped that Pepsi open, poured it over ice, and stuck a straw in it faster than the speed of light. Virginia started sipping away. After she finished wetting her whistle, she looked straight at me. Her eyes looked like blue crystal, so beautiful and sparking. Then she said, "Oh, Danielle, did I tell you that I went to Heaven?" "No, Virginia, tell me all about it," I replied. "Oh, it is so beautiful. An angel took me there," she continued. "The gates are huge and made of pearl, just stunning. All the streets are gold. The grass is a lush green, like velvet. When you walk on it, your footstep disappears and the grass comes right back up. There are beautiful colors everywhere, so vibrant. In the middle of every flower there is liquid gold. A bubbling brook runs through it and its crystal blue, so beautiful. There are mansions and the foundations of them are made of layers from different gems. There is music, beautiful singing coming from the throne of God. There is no fear, pain, or sadness there. Everyone is happy and full of love." As Virginia went on to describe Heaven and her experience, I almost felt badly for praying her back. Nevertheless, it was God's will for her to be around a while longer.

The doctor came in and was amazed and confused. He could not believe that she awakened and was chatting away. It was probably the next day Virginia was released and on her way home from her near-death experience. It was now two weeks after her release when we all sat around the table together eating raviolis and meatballs. I don't think I had ever seen Virginia chow down like that. I glanced over at Sharon and exchanged a smile as we witnessed Virginia's appetite. Sharon had that smile and a look that said, "Look what God has done!"

> *Mark 9:23: Jesus said to him, "If you can believe, all things are possible to him who believes."*

We were born to live in the supernatural and operate on a supernatural level. Jesus performed signs, wonders, and miracles. In His Word, He said we would do the same, and even greater things than these. "Impossible" is not an option according to His Word. We need to take the limits off our mind! We need operate from a heart of belief! That is, if God's Word says it, I believe it! In James 1:22 we are called to be doers of the Word, not hearers only! He needs us. He needs our mouths, our hands, and our feet to go where He sends us! We are in a revival of the supernatural, so get ready!

Wife and Mother Diagnosed with Cancer

I met Georgia Baker at a church I was a member of in Syracuse, New York. She was a pretty blonde lady who looked like she could be in a Dove soap commercial. Her personality was very endearing; she was friendly, warm, and always kind. She had two daughters. Then after a large span of time, she and her husband, Clayton, found out Georgia was pregnant again, this time with a boy. Clayton was a wonderful man as well, always kind, considerate, and very friendly. This was a great family with great representatives of Jesus Christ Who continually shined through them.

Two years after their son, David, was born, Georgia noticed a lump by her collarbone about the size of a pea. She wasn't too concerned about it, but Clayton wanted her to go to the doctor and get it checked out, so she made an appointment. The doctor wanted to run a few tests and MRI on the lump. Georgia was scheduled for a simple lymph node biopsy, which was supposed to take between a half hour to an hour. Clayton waited for Georgia's surgery to be complete. They had planned on eating lunch together afterwards. That lunch never happened.

Georgia woke up six hours later in an ambulance being rushed to the hospital to recover from extensive surgery. When the doctor went in to remove the lump, he found many affected nodules, and the surgery took hours. The surgeon went to the waiting room to speak to Clayton after the surgery and took a seat beside him. The doctor put his hands over his face and was very distressed. "Clayton, the reason the surgery went so long was because we found multiple affected lymph nodes. Are you familiar with melanoma?" he asked Clayton. "We are concerned that this is what it may be," the doctor continued. The doctor was particularly concerned because that very morning he had lost a close colleague to that aggressive cancer. It would take a week to get the results of the biopsy. Clayton was off to the hospital to be with Georgia. Now Clayton's mind was in a battlefield with the thoughts of possibly losing his wife, the woman he loved and the mother of his children.

When he arrived at the hospital they were fighting to stabilize Georgia from what was supposed to be a simple surgery. She was in and out of consciousness. Finally, Georgia woke, but it was touch and go for hours. When she came to her senses, she was asking, "What happened and why am I here?" The hospital room she resided in was cold and dark and she was scared. Then the scripture Psalm 23:4 came to her, "Yea, though I walk through the valley of the shadow of death, I will fear no evil; for You are with me…." She was definitely in the shadow of death, but Georgia was going to believe the Word of God and fear no evil. The next morning when she awoke, she was filled with great joy! All fear was gone! She knew whatever she was facing God was with her and that brought much comfort.

When Georgia and Clayton returned home, Georgia could sense the concern her children had for their mom. Clayton had not shared with her what the doctor had told him after her surgery. He didn't want to scare or upset her or maybe he just couldn't bring himself to repeat the bad report. On the inside Clayton was struggling to stay in faith. That Saturday evening they all snuggled up together in the family room. It was precious. A week would go by before the results of the biopsy.

Georgia was filled with joy and not even going to a place of defeat or the "what ifs." Clayton cared for Georgia, becoming her nurse, changing bandages and taking care of the household chores as he kept his secret regarding what the doctor had said. There was that seed of death and despair planted by the exchange of words between him and the surgeon. Clayton would turn to God in his prayers on behalf of his wife.

A week went by, and it was time to go to the surgeon's office to get the report. The doctor walked into the room, and although he was trying to have a bit of humor in his words, he appeared to be as white as a ghost. "Well, do you want the good news or the bad news first?" he asked. "The good news," Clayton and Georgia responded, of course, because they believe the "good news" of the gospel of Jesus Christ! "OK, the good news is, it's not melanoma." "Oh, thank God," Clayton let out a sigh. Then the surgeon continued, "The bad news is you have Hodgkin's lymphoma." A sense of peace came through the supernatural shield of faith that rose up within Georgia. No matter what the report, she had the joy of knowing that she would be healed. Again the scripture from Psalm 23:4 came up on the inside of her, "Yea, though I walk through the valley of the shadow of death, I will fear no evil;

for You are with me...." This was a pure evil report, but she was not going to fear it.

Georgia entered into prayer for her healing and stood on Psalm 23:4. That evening the door opened and fear started to grip her before she went to bed. Georgia slipped out of bed, knelt on her knees, and asked in her moment of weakness, "Lord, what did I do wrong?" but nothing came to her.

The next day was Sunday, time for church. Clayton, Georgia, and the children were off to Sunday service. At this point in time, Clayton and Georgia had not shared anything with anyone regarding this whole life-changing event. As Georgia stood worshipping the Lord in song, there came a tap on her shoulder. A woman who was behind her had a word from God and was being obedient to deliver it to her. "The Lord wants you to know you've done nothing wrong," the woman said. Warmth came over Georgia like oil; it blanketed her. She knew God was with her. This cancer wasn't because of sin, but for the glory of God! God had heard her prayer the night before and answered it through a vessel in church the next day. From that moment forward, Georgia rested in God's peace concerning the cancer.

Georgia was referred to an oncologist and was instructed to start chemo treatments. She checked in with the Lord about it and was directed to begin treatment. Without hesitation, she was obedient. A week following her first chemo treatment, Georgia became very sick with fever, nausea, a painful headache, and was unable to withstand light. She was admitted to the hospital on the palliative ward. That ward was where patients in their final stage were placed. The ward is decorated in a home-like setting to make the patients feel more comfortable in their surroundings in their last days. A barrage of tests followed: MRIs, spinal taps, etc.... No one could figure out what was causing the high fever and disabling headache Georgia was experiencing. A woman was placed on the ward who was in a coma, had kidney failure, and was given twenty-four hours to live. Patti, a friend of Georgia's, stopped by the hospital to visit her. While she was there, she was led to pray for the woman in the coma. After she did, the woman woke, started walking around, her kidneys were healed, and she went home twelve hours later. That woman was recorded as a medical miracle.

Georgia spent two weeks in the hospital before the symptoms cleared; they were unrelated to the chemo treatment. The symptoms that threatened to take Georgia's life were just a full-blown attack of the enemy. Georgia was a threat to the Kingdom, and the devil didn't like her. When she became well, she was dismissed, and she returned to her family.

After the incident of being hospitalized, which was unrelated to the chemo, the real reason for treatment would unfold. Nine months of chemo was scheduled for Georgia and that was a long time. She was informed of the side effects and what to expect: exhaustion, nausea, weakness, hair loss. When she began treatment, a wonderful thing happened! Georgia didn't experience any side effects besides a little sleepiness, but other wonderful things took place. When she would go in for treatments, God would send nurses, other patients, and family members to her to be encouraged and to be witnessed to. Georgia and Clayton became a light at the chemo treatment center. Everyone drew off the strength of the Lord in her, and she was the one diagnosed with cancer! Everyone looked forward to the Bakers coming to treatment because they were drawn to the light of Jesus within them. Georgia knew in the big picture this was a part of God's plan. This disease was not onto death. God had to get some things over to these people, and He used Georgia and Clayton to do it!

Halfway through treatment, approximately four months later, Georgia was declared completely clear! No more cancer! Her first reaction was, "No more chemo!" God working with Georgia killed it! Hallelujah! But the doctor encouraged her strongly to complete the other half of her treatment. She took it to the Lord. God revealed to her that when someone starts a race, they need to complete it. She was totally ready to stop treatment, but in obedience, she returned.

There were more people to be reached who needed to hear about God, His love, and healing power. She had prayed with a nurse in particular who was saved but had backslid. After speaking with Georgia, she rededicated her life to the Christ. There was a woman with stage-four breast cancer, and they prayed with her. A man with three months to live was ministered to. Little did Georgia know that even the doctor himself would be affected! In thirty-five years of practice, he had never seen a Hodgkin's patient have such victory!

This story can go on and on about all the individuals that were touched by God in this situation. Without God this would be terrifying to live out, but Georgia was determined to stand firm in the Word of God and His healing power. Today Georgia is cancer free and a healthy mom and wife. She has attained a new level of faith in God through this life-changing experience and God gets all the glory! Maybe as you read this today, you or someone you know is suffering with the effects of cancer. Today is the day that you can be released and healed, if you only believe. Healing is now in the supernatural. Sometimes it happens immediately. Sometimes it takes time to manifest. But the fact of the matter is you are healed!

If you or someone you know, needs healing now, pray this prayer. "Dear Heavenly Father, I thank You for Your son Jesus. I thank You that His blood was shed for me. I thank You, Jesus, that You died for my sin, sickness, and disease. I believe I am healed. I receive my salvation and my healing right now in the name of Jesus. Amen.

If you have prayed this prayer and received your answer, please email me at the email address at the end of my book. I would love to hear from you and share your report. Praise the Lord for He is good.

The Couple Who Wanted a Baby

I flew to Florida for my niece's wedding. It was to be held on the shore of the ocean with a reception to follow at a nearby hotel in a ballroom. My family and I were seated at a front table, and it was nice for all of us to be together at the same time.

I was there to enjoy my niece's wedding; I didn't think the Lord would use me there. Many people were drinking and getting a "buzz" on. Oh, how I remembered those days. I must admit, I prayed several times that some of these folks would make it home unharmed and that they wouldn't harm others. My brother, Dan, and I went to the dance floor and shared a dance, something we hadn't done since we were teenagers. Many of my family members are saved, which brings great comfort. I focused on enjoying my family and tried to block out some of the drunken people around me. Most of them were young people and the family of the groom. Typically, Christian weddings I have attended don't serve alcohol, but the groom and his parents were not saved and very much into alcohol, which concerned me regarding my niece.

I had just come off the dance floor with my brother, and as I settled into my seat, there was a tap on my shoulder. It was my sister Laureen and she had brought with her a man and a woman. She introduced me. They had French accents, and come to find out, they were originally from Canada. They both worked for my sister and brother-in-law in real estate. They were married and shared with me that they had been trying to get pregnant for seven years. They wanted a child so badly, and every avenue they tried failed. My sister told them when I came she would have me pray for them. I must admit, I was not prepared; this is what I call a cold call. This was a "be ready in season and out of season" situation. First I had to find out if they were saved. When I found out they were not, I began to witness to them. Yes, right there in the middle of drunks and a DJ playing loud music on the ballroom floor, they gave their hearts to Christ. Then we prayed, "Lord, open her womb. Prepare everything to work exactly how You designed it to, and bless them with a child." When we opened our eyes tears were streaming down their faces. They gave me a hug and were off to their seats. I sat down and thought, "Wow, Lord! You use the strangest times and places for your will to be done."

Three months later I got a call. The couple was pregnant—naturally! They were ecstatic! They got saved and then got pregnant. And it all started in the middle of a ballroom with loud music and intoxicated people at a wedding! I honestly had no idea that would take place that day. I almost couldn't make the wedding because of my schedule. It literally was a last minute thing. I was so thankful that God brought me there for this couple. I have learned always be ready, no matter where you are or what your doing. At any time, at any place, God will call you to be obedient and do what He tells you to do. This could have been the only opportunity for this couple to get saved and pregnant.

2 Timothy 4:2: Preach the Word! Be ready in season and out of season. Convince, rebuke, exhort, with all longsuffering and teaching.

The Road Trip

In a recent road trip to Illinois to visit my daughter and her family, I started out my 1,004-mile journey with my four-pound Yorkie named Bunny. I had high hopes of driving straight through, approximately sixteen hours with stops, but as the night fell, so did my stamina. I was looking for an exit with a hotel. I was nearly desperate to lay my head down and get a few hours of sleep before getting back on the road by early morning.

Finally, I found an exit with a hotel. I pulled off and cruised into the parking lot of what I thought would be my place of rest for the evening. In the parking lot were a couple of intoxicated individuals. A fight broke out and on the inside of me I knew this was not a safe place. As tired as I was, I headed back for the expressway.

Barely able to keep my eyes open, I anxiously watched for another opportunity to rest for the evening. I planned on maybe a six-hour stay, a shower, and to hit the road early in the AM. I noticed a welcoming sign that had a picture of a hotel, and I pulled off the highway again. As I approached the hotel, it was easy to tell it was new and much more tasteful. I was quite happy about the fact that the facility appeared fresh and clean, yet I didn't want to pay a high rate for a room that I would only spend six hours in.

I approached the desk and the clerk asked me if he could help me. "I just want a single room to rest for a few hours, take a shower, and get back on the road," I expressed. "Just a basic, simple room please." The desk clerk looked down at his computer and said, "The lowest price I have on a room is ninety dollars, plus tax and surcharges." "Ninety dollars?" I replied, slightly astounded. "Yes, that's right. Ninety dollars," he repeated. "I have my little four-pound dog with me," I slipped in. "That will be another twenty dollars for the dog," he added. "Oh, Lord," I thought. "You knew I would be staying here tonight. I am spent, so I trust you over my finances." Just then from behind, an arm rested over my shoulder and a hand was in my face. Two twenty-dollar bills were being waved in my face. I turned to see who was touching me and waving this money. There stood a stout middle-aged woman with short red curly hair. She was smiling. I asked her if she needed me to hand the money to the desk clerk for her. "No, this is for you," she said. "Huh, what do you mean?" I asked. She went on to tell me that she was in her hotel room watching television, and she heard on the inside of her that there was someone in the lobby who she was to give forty dollars. She came out to the lobby and I was the only one there, so she knew that someone was me.

She told me her house had recently burned down and they had lost everything except their lives. She felt very blessed to be alive. She expressed that the Lord blessed her and she wanted to be a blessing. In the middle of all her loss, she was giving. Wow! This was one obedient woman. "Thank you, I receive this blessing and may it be multiplied back to you," I replied. We hugged and exchanged a few words about God's goodness and she went back to her room.

Psalm 118:26: Blessed is he who comes in the name of the Lord.

I could tell by the desk clerk's face that even he was touched. I told the clerk I was going to get my dog out of the car. I didn't want her to feel abandoned. I could only imagine what her little mind was going through since I swept her away from her sisters and took only her for this long ride. I would peek over at her during my trip and I could see she was wondering, "What's going on?"

I grabbed Bunny and headed back to the front desk. Then the clerk said to me, "OK that will be twenty dollars for the night." "I thought I was paying fifty, plus twenty for Bunny after the forty dollars this lady had blessed me with?" I questioned. "No, I decided to give you a break on the room as well," he answered with a smile. (You see, the giving anointing jumped off of this lady and now onto the desk clerk. I love God's sense of humor.) "Thank you so much. You have no idea how much that blesses me."

"You will be in room 211. Here's the key," he said. "Do you have anything on the first floor, so I don't have to go up and down," I asked. "No, this room is right next to the elevator. You will like it much better. Trust me." OK," I thought. Don't look a gift horse in the mouth. I thanked him, grabbed my bag, and headed to the elevator. I stepped out of the elevator and there was my room, just like he said. It was the first room on the right, #211. Finally I could rest.

I slid my key in the slot, opened my door, and to my surprise, he had given me a big, beautiful suite! King size bed with a big, fluffy comforter, living room area, refrigerator, microwave, and a fancy tub! It appeared like no one had ever even been in the room besides me. "Oh, Bunny, look what God has blessed us with!" I plopped on the bed in amazement. Bunny snuggled up under my arm. "Look what just happened," I thought. God was mindful of me somewhere in Nebraska, meeting my needs, when I least expected it, from strangers no less!

> *Deuteronomy 28:3: "Blessed shall you be in the city, and blessed shall you be in the country."*

I don't need to be near home or around people who know me to be blessed. I am blessed in the city and in the country. That means anywhere I go. Only God could cause that to happen... only God. His hand is on everything in my life, even finding a hotel room. If I had stayed at the other hotel, I would have missed the blessing, and this lady and desk clerk would not have had the opportunity to be a blessing. "This is because you have been a blessing," I heard on the inside of me.

> *Philippians 4:19: And my God shall supply all your need according to His riches in glory by Christ Jesus.*

I took my shower, gave Bunny a bath, put on my pajamas and climbed under the fluffy comforter. My little dog tucked in the crook of my arm and was all snuggled in. I prayed that the Lord would multiply their giving and thanked Him for ordering my steps.

> *Psalm 115:12: The Lord has been mindful of us: He will bless us.*

Spirits and Principalities

I had been witnessing to a gentleman who spent eight years in prison for allegedly making gel bomb explosives used to blow up banks, to assist in bank robberies. He had turned his life around in prison and received a degree in a computer-related field. In a conversation one night, I inquired about his prison term and asked how he dealt with the confinement. He told me it was not too bad and that he would leave at night and go to different parts of the world through "astral projection." He described trips to Hawaii and other places. This sounded so foreign to me and so not God. He said there were other "spirits" that he would see in the atmosphere. This was the first time I had heard of anything of this sort. He was opposed to salvation. I tried many times, but he was a hard cookie to crack.

Often times at night, my daughter Niki would climb into my bed and talk. Then she would drift off to sleep. Even though she had her own room, she enjoyed dozing off with Mom now and then. One night after she fell asleep, I was in that pre-sleep stage when you are just falling into a sweet sleep…and then the strangest thing happened. As I was drifting off, out of nowhere it felt as though a light stream of electricity was circulating through my body as I lay there paralyzed. All of a sudden I sat up in my spirit, but my physical body was still lying down. I was a bit terrified and then all of a sudden—zip! I was completely out of my body and floating above it. As I looked down at my body and my daughter sleeping in the bed, I thought, "I'm dead!" I cried out, "Oh, God! No! Don't let me die with my daughter lying next to me! Please! This is not a memory I want her to have!" I pleaded with God. Then I heard, "You're not dying." I began to float to the corner of my bedroom toward the outside of our house. "Where am I going? What is happening?" I pleaded. Soon I was on the outside of my house and in the spirit world. "Oh, Heaven have mercy!" I cried out. This is the kingdom of the man I had been witnessing to, the one he entered into on a regular basis, was being revealed to me. What I was about to experience was the world he thrived in, and that is a scary place to be without Jesus.

What I witnessed would change my life forever. Right outside my house I had entered into the spirit world. There were thousands of spirits floating all around me. There were sounds coming from them that sounded like groaning and howling. They were floating to and fro looking for bodies to enter into. There were spirits of cancer, depression, sickness, disease, confusion, fornication, perversion, and much, much more. It was a dark, eerie, atmosphere and I did not like being there at all. I wanted out and I wanted out fast. I knew God was revealing to me the spirit world for a reason. This was the power that we battle against. They floated back and forth like vultures looking for a residency in persons unprotected in their minds, bodies, and spirits.

> *Ephesians 6:12: For we do not wrestle against flesh and blood, but against principalities, against powers, against the rulers of the darkness of this age, against spiritual hosts of wickedness in the heavenly places.*

"OK, God, I have seen enough! Return me to my daughter! I get it! I definitely get it!" I pleaded. I floated back into the bedroom and toward the bed. I hovered over my body for what felt like an eternity and then all of a sudden—zip! I was back in! I started praying in the spirit fervently. I rose out of my bed and went to the kitchen and got a bottle of olive oil and anointed my house and the doorways of our rooms. I prayed some more realizing the magnitude of the spiritual darkness that lurked outside. "Jesus, Jesus, Jesus!" I cried, and then it hit me. Not a single one of those spirits were in my house or felt invited to come in. All those evil spirits could do was float around it. My home and my daughter are covered in the blood of Jesus. Jesus' blood had power over them. My armor was Jesus' blood and the Word of God.

> *Ephesians 6:13-17: Therefore take up the whole armor of God, that you may be able to withstand in the evil day, and having done all, to stand. Stand therefore, having girded your waist with truth, having put on the breastplate of righteousness, and having shod your feet with the preparation of the gospel of peace; above all, taking the shield of faith with which you will be able to quench all the fiery darts of the wicked one. And take the helmet of salvation, and the sword of the Spirit, which is the word of God.*

Now I knew how these spirits operated, it is important for us to always guard our hearts and minds with the Word. I also am now very aware that when I see or meet someone whose mind is not whole or body is sick with disease, it is a spiritual stronghold. They need to be bound, rebuked, and covered in the blood, in Jesus name. This revelation came upon me in order to empower my ministerial gifts further, to cast out demons, and heal the sick.

What Is a Demon?

Satan who was the highest angel, rebelled against God. He was then cast out of heaven and took a third of the angels with him in rebellion. He was an angel called Lucifer. He was so in love with his own beauty, he fell into pride and self-centeredness. He thought he was bigger, better, and more powerful than the Almighty God.

> *Isaiah 14:12-14: "How you are fallen from heaven, O Lucifer, son of the morning! How you are cut down to the ground, You who weakened the nations! For you have said in your heart: 'I will ascend into heaven, I will exalt my throne above the stars of God; I will also sit on the mount of the congregation On the farthest sides of the north; I will ascend above the heights of the clouds, I will be like the Most High.'*

Satan was full of pride and pride caused his fall. Satan and his angels were now on a demonic mission to possess and take down as many people as possible. Demons torment people, possess them, lead them from God and His truth.

> *Mark 5:2-5: And when He had come out of the boat, immediately there met Him out of the tombs a man with unclean spirit, who had his dwelling among the tombs; and no one could bind him, not even with chains, because he had often been bound with shackles and chains. And the chains had been pulled apart by him, and the shackles broken in pieces; neither could anyone tame him. And always, night and day, he was in the mountains and in the tombs, crying out and cutting himself.*

"Cutting himself." Those words just shot into my heart as I am typing this scripture. I work with youth. I have been working with youth much of my saved life. I cannot tell you how many young people I have met that cut. It is very common in this day for trouble youth to cut themselves, and that is demonic! There is always a root to cutting that stems from their past. When identifying that root, teaching and counsel need to come into play and casting down that demonic stronghold is imperative. It's a cry for help and its identity needs to be uncovered, so it can be rebuked and healing can take its place.

> *V:6-9: When he saw Jesus from afar, he ran and worshiped Him. And he cried out with a loud voice and said, "What have I to do with You, Jesus, Son of the Most High God? I implore You by God that You do not torment me." For He said to him, "Come out of the man, unclean spirit!" Then He asked him, "What is your name?" And he answered, saying, "My name is Legion; for we are many."*

Demons torment people, possess them and lead them away from God and His truth. Expressions of demonic activity come in many forms such as lust of the flesh, gross perverted sexual practices, sadomasochism, pedophilia, drunkenness, gluttony, witchcraft. Mental disorders are forms of demonic strongholds, also the spirit of fear, hate, addictions, depression, fornication, and greed. They are all controlled by demons. When someone allows one demon in, that demon likes to invite his friends. You rarely find someone dealing with demon possession that is possessed by only one. There are many who love to jump on the bandwagon and join their buddies in an effort to torment and make their life a living hell, but God made a way of escape.

> *V:10-13: Also he begged Him earnestly that He would not send them out of the country. Now a large herd of swine was feeding there near the mountains. So all the demons begged Him, saying, "Send us to the swine, that we may enter them." And at once Jesus gave them permission. Then the unclean spirits went out and entered the swine (there were about two thousand); and the herd ran violently down the steep place into the sea, and drowned in the sea.*

We read in the scripture that Jesus had authority over the demons. There are more examples where Jesus exercised His authority over demon possession and cast the demons out. He has given us that same authority and dominion over them. We need to get a revelation of that power He placed inside of us through the Holy Spirit. We are supernaturally equipped just as Jesus was.

> *Luke 10:19: Behold, I give you the authority to trample on serpents and scorpions, and over all the power of the enemy, and nothing shall by any means hurt you.*

"Over all the power of the enemy," he has no power over us! None whatsoever! Wow! We need to get a hold of that and apply it in our call and purpose. That is powerful and supernatural! Demons flee at the name of Jesus.

Demons and Deafness

Following a powerful anointed message on healing and deliverance I preached at a church in Honduras, a woman made her way up to the altar. She spoke Spanish, but I had an interpreter translate what the woman was saying. The interpreter said that the woman was telling her that she had many seizures a day, sometimes over fifty. That is a lot of seizures! She was on medication, but even the medicine wouldn't help. The woman was at her wits' end and wanted it to stop. She had come to the altar to be healed. As the woman spoke, the Lord specifically showed me it was demon possession, and I was to pray and cast them out. I had two ladies with me who I had brought to the meeting to give their testimonies and share as well. They were standing with me when this woman with the seizures approached the altar.

Looking in this woman's eyes, I asked her through my interpreter if she believed Jesus could deliver her. She nodded yes. I had to take a different approach with this type of prayer; it was a prayer to cast out demons, and they can be nasty. I touched the woman's head and she began to immediately tremble, "Devils, I cast you out in the name of Jesus!" I commanded. The woman then had taken hold of both my arms and was digging her fingers in to my flesh with a lot of pressure. She began shaking out of control. I stood firm and told those demons I was not afraid of them because of the blood of Jesus. "Come out! Now!" I demanded. The woman started to foam at the mouth and then vomit. The ladies I had brought with me had eyes as big as potholes. They were holding on to her while trying to move their feet so as not to allow the vomit to hit them. All of a sudden the woman who only spoke Spanish, spoke in English. She sounded like an evil raspy man's voice and she said, "You can't get me!" "Oh, yes I can, devils! You come out in the name of Jesus!" The woman started jerking out of control, people had to scurry to get out of her way, "Come out! Come out!" I shouted as I followed her around. After much jerking and foaming she fell to the ground and just lay there completely paralyzed by God. Supernaturally the demons had come out!

> *Luke 9:1: Then He called His twelve disciples together and gave them power and authority over all demons, and to cure diseases.*

When she arose, she was peaceful, sweet and loving, and she was hugging me and thanking me that finally she had been delivered. She kept repeating, "Jesus, Jesus! Jesus!"

It wasn't by my power, but the power in me, the Holy Spirit that these demons had to flee. I was just a natural little lady doing God's work with the supernatural gifts He gave me. Sometimes I am awed that He uses ordinary people to perform these supernatural things.

Witnessing the power of God after the preaching of the Word, many began to make their way forward for prayer. Next there was a father who was holding his daughter's hand. She was seven. This little girl was born deaf. They had come to the altar believing that God would perform a miracle and let her hear. Well, that was all we needed: for them to believe that Jesus could do it. I placed my hands on her ears and commanded them to be open and hear!

Immediately the little girl could hear. I would say things in her ear in English and she would repeat them in English, over and over again. Her dad collapsed to the floor in tears: his prayers had been answered. Many more came forward, including the pastor and his wife. God answered many requests that day as everyone's faith was built up witnessing the mighty things that God had done.

On the way back to the hotel, the ladies were so taken back. They had never seen anything like that. They had read and heard about casting out demons and ears being opened, but never witnessed it. We chuckled at how dumb the devil is; it was a meeting to remember. They couldn't wait for the next opportunity for God to use them. I pray you are anticipating the next opportunity for God to use you as well.

Pray this prayer: "Dear Lord, You have chosen me. You have marked me with a mark. You have sanctified me with purpose and gifts. I ask that You would stir up the gifts within me. I will be obedient to do Your will. I will not limit myself with my natural capabilities, but I will glorify you with the supernatural power You have placed inside of me through the Holy Spirit. Amen."

The Toddler That Drowned

My son-in-law had a softball tournament that was out of town. The family drove to the tournament and rented a hotel room. At the time, NayNay was about eight months pregnant with her fourth child. My three grandchildren were with them. Zoe had brought along her cousin, Julie, and her friend, Nikki. Zoe was ten at the time, Nikki was eleven, and Julie was about twelve.

My son-in-law had left that morning for the game. Around 10 AM the girls asked NayNay if they could go to the pool to swim. She said no at first, since it was so early in the day, but the girls kept pushing for a yes. Finally, NayNay agreed, and they got their swimsuits on and went to the pool at the hotel. They were the only persons at the pool that morning, or so they thought. NayNay sat at the kiddy pool with my grandsons. Zoe, Nikki, and Julie went to swim in the big pool.

A few minutes passed when Zoe went to Nay and said, "Mom, there is a boy under the water and he has been down there a really long time." "Maybe he wants to see how long he can hold his breath," she answered. "No, Mom, he's been there a really long time and he's not in a natural position," Zoe replied. Then it hit Nay, "Grab him! Grab him!" she yelled. As the girls retrieved the boy, Nay ran to the front desk to call 911.

The girls laid the unconscious boy on the side of the pool. His lips were purple, and they put their hands on him and began to pray over him. All of a sudden Julie got baptized in the Holy Ghost while praying. Then out of nowhere a man appeared, knelt beside the boy, and turned him on his side. When he had done this, a lot of water came out of the boy's mouth and then the unidentified man disappeared. The boy still lay unconscious.

NayNay had returned and the medics arrived. They were working on the child. Then the mother came in frantic and crying. While they were working on the boy, NayNay calmed the mother and asked if she could pray for her son. She prayed with the woman asking that her son would be healed and that he would be completely whole in Jesus name. Still unconscious, the child was taken to the hospital where he was placed in ICU. It turned out the boy's mom and her family were having a family reunion, and she thought her son was with his aunt, and the aunt thought he was with his mother. It wasn't neglect, just an unfortunate misunderstanding.

NayNay took the children back up to the room in order to keep out of the medics' way. While in the room, they heard voices outside and stepped out on the terrace to see who it was. A crowd of people had gathered and when they saw them, they pointed toward the girls and said, "That's them! That's the girls that saved the boy!" Julie turned to NayNay and said, "Aunt Nay, can I just tell them something?" "Sure," she replied. Then NayNay announced to the crowd, "My niece would like to say something." Everyone got quiet. Now Julie was bit of a quiet, shy girl, so this was an unusual request.

Julie looked down at the crowd and said, "It wasn't us who saved that little boy today. It was God. God prompted us to go to the pool." She continued, "Jesus loves that boy, and He loves you and wants to be your Lord too." The crowd began to cheer and clap. They stepped back inside their room. "Aunt Nay, I don't know where those words came from, but that was not me talking," Julie stammered. "That was God speaking through you, Julie," Nay explained.

The police arrived and the chief of police was one of them. They took the report from the girls who reaffirmed that God prompted them to be there. After taking the report, he said to them, "I don't know that this would happen, but you girls deserve a heroic reward." However the girls knew it was God and not they. A few months later, the girls received a junior hero award from the VFW. Most importantly, a toddler was saved, a mother had her child, and he was completely whole. Thanks are to God!

Divine appointments: God has them mapped out for us. Yes, He uses children as well. He will use anyone willing. In this instance it was a couple of young girls. God uses any believer who is obedient and willing. These girls were just exemplifying what they were taught, knew, and believed. Age doesn't matter to God; obedience and belief are what matters. These children acted upon their belief system and a miracle took place! The boy lived and had no brain damage after being without oxygen for so long. God answered the prayer of the girls, Nay, and the boy's mom! We believe the unidentified man was an angel. Praise the Lord!

Please Don't Let My Baby Die

On July 19, 2004, I got that call that every mother fears. It was about 6:15 PM when the phone rang. I picked up and said, "Hello." I could hear sirens and radio gargle in the background. On the other end of the phone was my son-in-law. "Danielle, I need to know if Nay is allergic to anything?" he asked. "Why?" I questioned. "I just need to know," he replied. "Why can't you ask her yourself?" I inquired. "Danielle, I just need to know," he said pointedly. "Just bee stings." "Is she OK?" I asked. "I will call you in thirty minutes," he responded. I could feel the blood drain from my face and I became woozy. "What's wrong?" John asked. "Something horrible, very, very horrible," I stammered. "I need to pack a bag! Quick! Call the airline! I need to get out on the next flight!"

"Hurry, help! I need help! I can't think! I can't think!" I said frantically. I was trying to keep my thoughts straight but to no avail. John was scurrying, packing my bags. I knew if my daughter wasn't talking, it was bad.

My daughter and her family were living in Montana, and we were currently living in Oklahoma at the time. I was waiting for the phone to ring, so I could be informed of what happened. That was the slowest thirty minutes I had ever experienced in my life, but no call. Forty minutes, no call... forty-five minutes, no call. Finally I called my son-in-law's phone, but he didn't answer. His sister did. "What's going on with NayNay?" I asked. The answer I wanted to hear did not come. "Well, Danielle, there's been an accident. They were holding down the children's trampoline in a windstorm by sitting on it. It flipped over to the neighbor's house. The wind took NayNay and the trampoline up, and then it slammed her into the ground. She is unconscious." "Well, how serious is it?" I questioned. "She could die," were her words that sunk my heart. "OK, I will be on the first flight out," I stammered. "Well, call me and I will pick you up at the airport. They are sending an airplane with a trauma crew to pick her up. It's too windy for a helicopter. They are taking her to Great Falls. There's an ICU Head Trauma Unit there." I called the airline and they got me on the first flight out in the morning. There was nothing available besides that flight. I knew it was going to be a long night.

"Please! Please! Please! God don't let her die," I cried out as I knelt to my knees. I was either on my knees or pacing and praying from the moment I hung up the phone. I fell asleep from exhaustion around 4:45 in the morning. I was a wreck—I won't deny it. Then the voice of reasoning from the Holy Spirit would come in, "Come on, Danielle, you know it's not God's will for your daughter to die and leave those three babies behind." Then fear would grip again, and it was disabling. I couldn't fix it. Then the Holy Spirit would speak on the inside, "You know the Word of God. This is not His will, nor did He cause it." Then back to fear—I don't think I have ever felt such a roller coaster of emotions in such a short period of time. I couldn't pack, I couldn't think straight, I couldn't talk, and I felt paralyzed emotionally. I just wanted to be on that plane! I just wanted to see my girl! I wanted to touch her and tell her how much I love her! The last conversation I had with her kept rolling through my mind. It was a good one. We were very close and we always closed our phone calls with, "I love you."

Ever since the day I got saved, I stood in the gap for healing, miracles, raising of the dead with undefeatable faith. But now it was close to home. It was my child! This was different, because it was personal! I was out of control and was struggling to get it back. I knew I would do her no good this way. In the morning I grabbed my anointing oil and stuck it in my pocket. We were off to the airport. Tears were streaming down my face. Although I was happy she made it through the night, I couldn't control the tears. My mind was in a battlefield, and I didn't like all the places I was going in my thoughts. I fought to get in faith and then minutes later, was back out of faith. "I have to stay in faith!" I would tell myself over and over.

I boarded the plane feeling completely exhausted and emotionally distraught. The person I sat next to kept handing me tissues. I didn't tell her what happened. I couldn't even talk. She could tell something was terribly wrong. The flight attendant kept asking me if there was anything she could do. All I could do was shake my head, no. I knew the only one who could help was God. "Why," I wondered. "Why?" I asked. Then I was directed by God not to ask that question. "OK." I whispered to Him. "I will trust You."

I finally arrived at the airport in Great Falls; I was picked up. The ride to the hospital was very strained. I just wanted to get there and see my girl. Finally we arrived at the hospital and took the elevator to ICU. I was taken to my daughter's room where she lay in a bed on an ice sheet to keep her hypothermal to reduce brain swelling. On the right front side of NayNay's skull was a port where a hole had been drilled to measure cranial pressure, and there was also a lot of swelling. I had also found out that her pelvis was fractured as well. In my daughter's mouth was a tube, providing her with oxygen, and in her tummy, another tube to feed her. In her right arm was an IV to provide her with fluids. All around her she was surrounded by machines lit up, blinking and beeping. She lay there motionless, her eyes closed, but bulging out from the swelling in her head. I picked up her hand. It was motionless with no life in it. "Baby, it's Momma," I said, but no response. I felt like I was going to collapse.

The next morning we had a conference with Dr. G., my daughter's neurosurgeon, to update us on her condition. We all sat around an oval table in a conference room in the ICU wing. Dr. G. said that a brain response test they had done to try to stimulate her limbs showed no response from her brain. The whole thing felt surreal, like I was in a movie. This couldn't be happening. They even asked if she is an organ donor. Although this is a common question asked when a family member is in the ICU, as a mother, I was not prepared to hear or think about that option. The doctor said she might never wake up. If she did, there was a good possibility she would be mentally and physically handicapped. One nurse even used the word "vegetable," referring to my precious daughter.

Finally reality hit me: there is nothing the medical world could do to save my daughter. Only God could do that. By the third day in, I was prepared to fight the fight of faith. I hit my knees often in the little chapel on the first level of the hospital, and God always met me there. Every day, I would go to my daughter's side and anoint her with frankincense and myrrh oil. I had my Bible with me at all times and read repeatedly, all the different ways Jesus healed in Matthew chapters eight and nine. I read to my daughter over and over again, healing scriptures. I spoke over her repeatedly that she would live to raise her three children. My repeated chant to my daughter became, "Nay, it's Momma, open your eyes for Momma—I want to see those beautiful, green eyes," but nothing. Not even a flutter of an eyelash. I turned to the Word of God constantly, building up my faith. I also read and re-read *The Power of Positive Thinking,* by Norman Vincent Peale, a book that encourages you to think and speak positively with faith. I stopped going to doctor conferences after the third day because the reports were always bad.

I was reading the Bible on the third day, and I came across a chapter that I had read a hundred times or more, but it shot out at me like an arrow to my heart. It was the story of Lazarus.

> *John 11:1-3: Now a certain man was sick, Lazarus of Bethany, the town of Mary and her sister Martha. It was that Mary who anointed the Lord with fragrant oil and wiped His feet with her hair, whose brother Lazarus was sick. Therefore the sisters sent to Him, saying, "Lord, behold, he whom You love is sick."*

> *V:6-8: So, when He heard that he was sick, He stayed two more days in the place where He was. Then after this He said to the disciples, "Let us go to Judea again." The disciples said to Him, "Rabbi,*

lately the Jews sought to stone You, and are You going there again?"

V:11-15, 17: These things He said, and after that He said to them, "Our friend Lazarus sleeps, but I go that I may wake him up." Then His disciples said, "Lord, if he sleeps he will get well." However, Jesus spoke of his death, but they thought that He was speaking about taking rest in sleep. Then Jesus said to them plainly, "Lazarus is dead. And I am glad for your sakes that I was not there, that you may believe. Nevertheless let us go to him." So when Jesus came, He found that he had already been in the tomb four days.

Ding! Ding! Ding! Whistles! Bells! The lights came on here for me. Major revelation from a story I had read and even preached portions of came to light! Lazarus was dead and in the grave four days! No brain activity and no breath in his lungs for days! No breathing tube! No ice sheets! No port in his skull! Lazarus was just flat out dead! Is not Jesus the same? Yesterday, today, and forever! He changes not! I read on.

V:17: So when Jesus came, He found that he had already been in the tomb four days.

Four days dead! Four days wrapped up in grave clothes!

V:20-23: Now Martha, as soon as she heard that Jesus was coming, went and met Him, but Mary was sitting in the house. Now Martha said to Jesus, "Lord, if You had been here, my brother would not have died. But even now I know that whatever

You ask of God, God will give You." Jesus said to her, "Your brother will rise again."

V:32, 33: Then, when Mary came where Jesus was, and saw Him, she fell down at His feet, saying to Him, "Lord, if You had been here, my brother would not have died." Therefore, when Jesus saw her weeping, and the Jews who came with her weeping, He groaned in the spirit and was troubled.

Jesus was grieved because of their unbelief.

V:34, 35: And He said, "Where have you laid him?" They said to Him, "Lord, come and see." Jesus wept.

Jesus wept because of their lack of faith. He was able to raise Lazarus from the dead. They didn't believe that He the Son of God, who was filled with power, was able to raise Lazarus. The people thought Jesus wept because he was sad to know Lazarus had died. This was not true. Jesus knew he had the power to raise him. He was saddened that the belief system of the people was so futile.

V: 38-45; Then Jesus, again groaning in Himself, came to the tomb. It was a cave, and a stone lay against it. Jesus said, "Take away the stone." Martha, the sister of him who was dead, said to Him, "Lord, by this time there is a stench, for he has been dead four days." Jesus said to her, "Did I not say to you that if you would believe you would see the glory of God?" Then they took

> *away the stone from the place where the dead man was lying. And Jesus lifted up His eyes and said, "Father, I thank You that You have heard Me. And I know that You always hear Me, but because of the people who are standing by I said this, that they may believe that You sent Me." Now when He had said these things, He cried with a loud voice, "Lazarus, come forth!" And he who had died came out bound hand and foot with graveclothes, and his face was wrapped with a cloth. Jesus said to them, "Loose him, and let him go." Then many of the Jews who had come to Mary, and had seen the things Jesus did, believed in Him.*

Wow! I had another level of faith take residency in me by re-reading that story. Jesus would do for my daughter what He had done for Lazarus. If I only believe, I would see the glory of God. He didn't need anything but faith. My faith confession became this, "My daughter will rise up and be whole, nothing missing, nothing broken, complete restoration." However, despite the faith going up from thousands of people all over the world, her physical condition was not changing, except for the worse. But my faith confession changed not. I sat in my daughter's room day after day, repeating my confession. I read scripture to her and talked to her as though she was able to hear and comprehend everything I was saying. I even gave her a manicure. I kissed her face hundreds of times and told her she was healed. I fasted for her life.

Around the fifth day, when other family members came to visit, I went down to the chapel. I spent many times over the last five days in that chapel, on my knees, but this time it was different. When I stepped inside, I was immediately in the presence of God. I dropped to my knees and prayed a prayer that went like this, "Lord, I know it's Your will for my daughter to live, but I want You to know, that if You were to have taken her, I would still serve You." Something clicked in the Spirit; I knew it immediately. It was what He was looking for from me. Those words turned a switch; I knew that He wanted to know that from me. The presence of God was so strong at that moment that all I could do was kneel there silently and soak in His presence. It reminded me of when I had dropped to my knees some twenty-seven years earlier. My same daughter was dying of a rare blood disease and I said this prayer, "Jesus, I don't even know how to pray, but please don't let my baby die." He healed her and I got saved. Oh, how comforting it was to have Him right there with me in that chapel. He filled my soul with peace.

On my way back to my daughter's room I met Dr. G. in the hallway and he stopped me. "Danielle, how come you haven't been in the morning conferences?" he asked. My thoughts were, "He is going to think I am wigged out when I tell him the answer." The nurses and staff thought I had false hope and lost my mind. I had to be true to my confession of faith, though, so I told him. "Dr. G., I just can't go in and listen to the negative reports. It's interfering with my faith," I answered. "What are you believing for, Danielle?" he asked. "I am believing that my daughter will wake up and be whole, nothing missing, nothing broken, complete restoration," I proclaimed. Dr. G. reached out his hands toward me and said, "Give me your hands; I am going to stand in faith with you." And together we prayed a prayer of agreement, the neurosurgeon and myself. Praise the Lord!

> *Matthew 18:19-20: "Again I say to you that if two of you agree on earth concerning anything that they ask, it will be done for them by My Father in heaven. For where two or three are gathered together in My name, I am there in the midst of them."*

Another level of faith immediately took place after that prayer. It was awesome to have the doctor who is caring for my girl to be hooked up in faith with me for a miracle!

My sisters flew in from Brooklyn and Florida. It was comforting to have them there. One day we decided to go out and see my grandchildren. The children hadn't seen their mother in days. Although I didn't want to leave my daughter's side, I knew it was important for me to spend time with them.

My sisters and I drove to see the children. My sisters are hilarious Italians, especially when the three of us are together. A bunch of Italian women can make a normal activity action packed. When we arrived, the children were so excited to see us. The baby, just a little over one year old, was in his aunt's arms. We played with the kids and then took my granddaughter and grandson out to Walmart. We all needed a little fun. We filled up our carts with Batman everything and girlie stuff for Zoe. It was just a light fun time for the kids and us. Lunch was at Burger King by the children's request and then we headed back to the house.

When we got back, I picked up the phone to call ICU and see how my daughter was doing. "She is having a good day," said the nurse. "Yah! Nay is having a good day!" I announced after I hung up the phone. "What does that mean?" Zoe asked. Zoe had not mentioned the accident since it happened.

She didn't want to discuss it and she would not ask questions. "Well, Zoe, it means that things were not getting worse, and that your mom is doing well today," I replied. Everyone was quiet. No one was saying a word. What would we tell her? That was the question in all of our minds. Then Zoe spoke again, "I don't care if my Mom is in a wheelchair for the rest of her life. I just want to know if she will have the same personality?" What a precious question that was. More than anything she loved her mom's personality. Silence fell in the room now. Then faith rose up in me and I answered, "Zoe, your mom will not be in a wheelchair and she will have her personality." Zoe's face lit up, she put her arms around my neck and said, "I love you, Nanny." That was totally a faith statement I made to my granddaughter. I had to confess by faith the supernatural outcome of my daughter's accident to my granddaughter. "This is a biggie, God. I just told my little granddaughter her mommy will be whole. I believe You can pull this off, Lord, and we will give You the glory."

On the seventh day, still no change in the natural. I had done all I knew how to do. I read the Word every day. I anointed my daughter with oil so many times that her room smelled like a temple in the Old Testament. It was a great fragrance that emitted the reminder of the faith we were standing in for her miracle.

In the midst of everything going on with my girl, God kept sending people in my path who didn't know Him. Some were staff members, some were family members who had relatives in ICU. I ended up witnessing every day and bringing three new souls into the Kingdom of God. Sometimes at what seems to be our lowest low, God wants to see if we will be obedient and I was. Looking back, part of the reason I was there was to encourage and bring others to Christ.

The seventh day had arrived, and doing all I knew to do, I was exhausted. I hadn't eaten and I was feeling the physical strain. When you have done all you know how to do, just stand and keep standing. Don't waver! If we wavered we would lose her. Just stand!

I stayed with my daughter all day, speaking to her, speaking over her. I just wanted to see her eyes. I had asked her a thousand times to open her eyes. NayNay has the most beautiful eyes. They are big, almond shaped and the prettiest hazel green—just captivating. When she was a baby, I would just stare into those eyes and behold them as she would suck away at her bottle. Her expressions with those eyes told a story. You would always know what was going on with NayNay just by looking into those eyes. Oh, how I longed to see them again. I kissed my daughter goodnight. My son-in-law was there, and he would stay the whole night. It was off to my hotel room, which was right across the street from the hospital.

I slipped on my pajamas, took a few sips of water, and tried to get comfortable in my bed. Since the accident, I had not had one full night of sleep. Waking four to five times a night was becoming common and was starting to take a toll on my body and mind. Between fasting and not sleeping, my mind was starting to feel like I was in a fog. I closed my eyes and hoped that this would be the night I would sleep all the way through. I tossed and turned. I just couldn't turn off my brain. Finally, I got up out of my bed and hit my knees to pray. This had become a common occurrence for me. This time my prayer went like this: "Lord, I know it's Your will for my daughter to be healed, completely restored, nothing missing, nothing broken. I don't mean to fleece You, Lord, but I just want to see her eyes. Please, would You just let me see her beautiful eyes?" As I prayed that prayer, I felt the anointing. It felt like warm oil soaking my entire body. He heard me and He was there with me, again. I opened my eyes and there in my room was a glory cloud. I cried, not out of fear or sadness, but out of the realization of His awesomeness. Finally, I climbed into bed, pulled up the covers, and slept like a baby. I knew He heard my prayer, and I knew He would answer it.

The next morning I woke up refreshed. I slept like a baby! I took a shower, put on a fresh outfit of clothes and walked over to the hospital with a smile on my face. I just knew I would see her eyes open that day! I walked into NayNay's room and her nurse and respiratory therapist were there. "Good morning," I said. "Good morning," said the nurse. "We are looking mighty chipper this morning. What do we owe this to?" she asked. "My daughter is going to open her eyes today!" I exclaimed. She glanced over at the respiratory therapist as if to say, "She has really lost her mind now." I knew she thought I was in denial that past week and had gone over the deep end with my faith confession. "What makes you think she will open her eyes?" she asked. "God," I answered. Another glance toward each other as if to say, "This lady needs a shot of reality." "Well, if God told you that, why don't you try to get her to open her eyes," she replied. She was hoping I would have a wake-up call. All I knew was I had an encounter with God last night. He heard my prayer, and He was going to answer it. My faith was up for the challenge. Now they were both looking at each other as if to say, "This will be interesting." Not one fiber within either one of them believed her eyes would open.

I stepped up to my daughter's head. She looked like Sleeping Beauty with her long, dark hair and her long, thick, black eyelashes. I leaned toward her ear. "It's Momma, Baby. Open up your eyes. Momma wants to see those beautiful green eyes." Everything was quiet in the room as I prompted her. Then it happened! Her eyelashes fluttered, she opened her eyes, and she had a dead lock stare right into my eyes.

Her eyes looked different, like green crystal, as though you could see right into her soul. She stared at me and then her lips began to quiver, just like they would when she was a little girl. "It's OK Baby," I said. Tears started streaming down her face, and then she mouthed the word, "Mom." She began to repeat my name over and over. She had a tracheotomy in place now, so it was difficult to put sound to it, but you could clearly see that she recognized me and was saying my name. "She recognizes me!" I kept repeating. If she were brain dead, she wouldn't know who I was. The funny thing was, she was so focused on me that she wasn't aware of the nurse or the therapist. They were now holding their chests and looked like they'd seen a ghost. Her cranial pressure was rising, so I began to encourage her to go to sleep. It took twenty minutes, but she finally drifted off. Dr. G. had already done his rounds and left for the day. That was OK because God had answered my prayer and showed Himself real to the ladies in the room. I was a happy mom.

Later that afternoon around 3:00 PM, a family member came to visit my daughter. The nurse was in the room. She wanted some privacy, so I left to go to the waiting room. As I walked down the hallway of ICU, a hand grabbed my shoulder and spun me around. It was the nurse. "Where are you going?" she demanded, "Well, I was going to give them some alone time," I responded. "You get back in that room. Dr. G. is on his way here and he wants you in that room!"

she said sternly. "OK," I said and I turned and headed back toward the room.

Once I got back to the room, staff members and family members started to file in and surround my daughter's bed. I took a seat on the recliner allowing others to visit. In walked Dr. G. He was about 6'3" and a slender man who held himself with confidence. He was scanning the room with his eyes. He finally spotted me and said, "Mom, I heard you woke your daughter up today!" "No, Dr. G., God woke my daughter, not me," I said. "Well, let's see if God will do it again!" Dr. G. had come all the way back to the hospital because he was called and told NayNay opened her eyes. He walked over to her feet and was shaking them, asking her to wake up, but no results. Then he stepped up to her ear, "Nay, wake up!" No response. Then he looked at me and said, "Mom, come over here and wake your daughter up." As I rose and walked to my daughter, my internal conversation with God was, "Oh, Lord, before all these witnesses, show them you are real." I leaned toward my girl and repeated the words, "NayNay, it's Momma. Open your eyes for Momma. I want to see those beautiful green eyes." Her eyelashes fluttered, and then she did it again! She opened her eyes, and everyone gasped. Again her lips quivered as tears streamed down her face. Her eyes were fixated on me and she began to mouth my name over and over. "You're OK Baby. You just need to get some rest. Everything is fine," I reassured her. Dr. G. had me see if she could move her fingers and toes. Her arms and legs quivered, so we could see she was trying to get the message to them, but she couldn't get them to move. "OK, OK, tell her to go back to sleep. Her cranial pressure is rising," he said. I tried to get her to sleep. It took a while, but she finally did.

She was in a coma for a few more weeks before it was time for her to wake up. She didn't have all her memory at first. She thought she was a teenager. She didn't know she was married and had kids, but things would come back and trigger her memory. She was sent to rehab where they estimated she could be there for six months to a year. She had to re-learn everything. She checked out of rehab in five weeks!

Today my daughter is completely restored, nothing missing, nothing broken. She owns three coffee businesses and had a fourth child with her husband.

She was a gifted child. In her school years, she attended the gifted program. A year and a half after the accident, they retested her IQ and it was ten points higher than the last time she was tested. She had complete restoration and some extra good stuff included! God is a miracle-working God, and He honors our faith.

> *Hebrews 11:1, 6: Now faith is the substance of things hoped for, the evidence of things not seen. But without faith it is impossible to please Him, for he who comes to God must believe that He is, and that He is a rewarder of those who diligently seek Him.*

When you are standing in faith for anything, don't waver. We all want immediate results and sometimes we do get immediate results, but when we don't, we just have to stand. Read the Word. Confess the Word. Anoint with oil. Speak in faith, as though it is already done, and believe! He is able to perform what His Word says He will do. Then just stand and stand some more. It will come to pass.

The supernatural ability of God is inexplicable. It requires an important element: faith. With faith all things are possible. Nothing is impossible to God.

In Conclusion

My hope in writing this compilation of true stories is to show the revelation of the fact that God has filled us with supernatural power. On the day we accepted Jesus Christ as our Lord and Savior, He filled us with power through the Holy Spirit. Reading the Bible, we learn of all the ways Jesus healed, performed miracles, raised the dead and acquired believers. Most interestingly is what the Word says about us as believers, and that is that we have that same power to perform the things Christ did.

> *John 14:12-14: Most assuredly, I say to you, he who believes in Me, the works that I do he will do also; and greater works than these he will do, because I go to My Father. And whatever you ask in My name, that I will do, that the Father may be glorified in the Son. If you ask anything in My name, I will do it.*

Administering healing, miracles, and raising of the dead are the rights we acquired from our Heavenly Father. Don't ever let failure, doubt, or "impossible," enter your thoughts. These thoughts are opposite of what the Word says about you. Know your rights, possess them, and go and produce for the Kingdom of God. Know that He is working with you. Signs and wonders follow the preaching of the Word. We are called to do works beyond the laws of the natural, just as Jesus demonstrated in His life.

If you have a story to share or would like to contact Danielle you may do so by mail, phone, email or website.
Danielle DeMartino
Phone 720-335-3416
1804 Downing Ave.
Westchester, Illinois 60154
Email: danielle.demartino@yahoo.com
Website: DanielleDeMartino.com

CPSIA information can be obtained at www.ICGtesting.com
Printed in the USA
LVOW072038110313

323738LV00003B/9/P